IT DOESN'T MATTER WHAT YOU KNOW

... UNLESS YOU CAN *COMMUNICATE* WHAT YOU KNOW!

Practical Presentation
Guidelines for Getting
Your Ideas Across

SHERRY M. WYATT

Wheless-Wyatt Communications
www.wheless-wyatt.com

ISBN: 1475122969
ISBN 13: 9781475122961

Special thanks to

Bill Wheless

*Bits of his wit and wisdom appear throughout this book.
He taught me everything I know,
and I will be forever grateful.*

Table of Contents

Introduction

You don't know what you don't know. That accurately describes my career before I landed in the communications business. I mention it because I suspect it may be true for you, as well.

As with most people, my days were filled with interactions with other people. Many of the experiences were fulfilling and even inspiring. Yet, too many were just the opposite. Why was it so difficult to get my ideas across, to have people understand me, to want to partner with me, to see things my way? Why were there so many misunderstandings? Why were we constantly doing things over, getting things wrong, wasting so much time?

I enjoyed many years in the television broadcasting business contributing by bringing in advertising clients whose revenue supported the station. If I had only known then what I know now about communication, how much more successful I would have been!

What I have learned is that everything is dependent on effective communication. No matter what your job, communication is over 90 percent of what you do. When you speak so people will listen and listen so people will speak, misunderstandings will be eliminated, relationships will be enhanced, and your success will sky rocket.

This book is not just about creating and delivering presentations. It's about communication. The skills you use in front of an audience are the same skills you use when interacting one-on-one. In both scenarios, you are expected to be clear, concise, logical, persuasive, interesting.

I Don't Do Speeches or Stand-up Presentations. Is This Book For Me?"

Well, let's see.

Are you a leader or manager of a company, team, or group?

If so you are expected to:

- have a vision and clearly pass that vision on to those who report to you

- motivate and inspire those around you through your communication skills

- represent your company or group professionally, internally, and to the board of directors (if you have one) and to your clients, potential clients, and the public

- stay up to date and informed and speak from a depth of knowledge clearly, concisely, and authoritatively

Are you a member of a team or group?
If so you are expected to:

- think and have an opinion you can clearly share with others by developing the skill of disciplined thinking and speaking in a logical, easy-to-follow manner

- communicate with your colleagues in a manner that adds value to the time they spend listening to you

- listen actively in all communication situations and therefore eliminate miscommunications and reduce the 60 percent of business errors caused by poor listening

Are you in sales, responsible for bringing income into your organization?
If so you are expected to:

- represent your organization by presenting yourself in a professional and efficient manner

- exhibit that you maintain a current base of knowledge about your products and industry and your clients' industries

- communicate with your clients in a manner that inspires trust and results in their wanting to do business with you

- present your products and services in an accurate and interesting manner that addresses the needs of your customers

- exhibit traits that make you stand out from your competition as a trusted partner and not just another vendor

Are you in research, reporting, or financial analysis for your company?
If so you are expected to:

- communicate to senior management, your board of directors, stockholders, the media, the public, and others in your organization

- have the skills to present complex technical or financial data in a clear, easy-to-understand manner while demonstrating your knowledge and competence

Are you an employee, a colleague, a friend, a spouse or significant other, or a parent? In other words, are you a human being?
If so you are expected to:

- respond when spoken to

- listen effectively

- interact with those around you and communicate in a clear, concise, interesting, and understandable manner

- be engaged

Communication accounts for 90 percent of all that you do. You don't have to aspire to be a professional speaker to find value in this book. All good communication requires you to be clear, concise, interesting, and persuasive. The ideas you will learn in this book are applicable to any communication situation in which you find yourself. Replace the word "audience" with "anyone on the other side of you," apply the concepts, and communicate in a manner that inspires confidence and trust.

Otherwise, it really doesn't matter what you know..........

Part 1 - Before You Step In
Front of an Audience

◇◇

Human interaction is the basis for life as we know it. People are connected to one another through feel-ings—whether good, bad, or indifferent. Our feelings develop from our impressions of one another. If you want those around you to have a positive impression of you, to understand you, to agree with you, to rally and support you, to be inspired by you, and to react in a way that gets you what you want, then you must **com-municate** in a manner that generates those outcomes.

> *"The #1 criterion for advancement and promotion for professionals is an ability to communicate effectively."*
>
> *—Harvard Business Review*

The goal of this book is to provide a step-by-step, clearly defined guide to developing the skills of effective communication and presentation. You will learn how to communicate with confidence, clarity, and purpose.

You will learn that to be a good presenter, you must be a disciplined thinker and an effective communicator in all your interactions with other people. A communicator "transmits or reveals a feeling or thought by speech, writing, or gesture so that it is clearly understood" (*Encarta Dictionary*).

Isn't clear understanding the responsibility of the listener? Hardly. You see, **it doesn't matter what you know unless you can communicate what you know to another person or persons to their level of understanding and, as a result, make something happen.** Your success (or lack of it) in business and in life is based on how you interact with other people—in other words, how you communicate.

> *"You can have brilliant ideas, but if you can't get them across, your ideas won't get you anywhere."*
>
> —Lee Iacocca, executive, author

What does how you communicate with other people have to do with how you present? The words are interchangeable. A good presenter has a conversation with his or her audience, either verbally or implied. He or she gets his or her ideas across and reads their faces and reacts to what he or she sees. A good presenter brings the audience around to his or her way of thinking by understanding them, educating them, persuading them, and leading them. Ideas and feelings flow back and forth.

The skills you use in any communication situation are the same skills you use in every communication situation. You are expected to be clear, focused, interesting, logical, concise, persuasive, motivating, inspiring, knowledgeable, and convincing.

Think about it. Does it really matter whether you are speaking to one person or one thousand people? The goal is the same—to influence the outcome.

Of course, over the lunch table, your gestures won't be quite as large; your voice won't be quite as loud. The skills that make you successful in a lunch-table discussion, however, are the same skills that will help you move an audience.

Self-Awareness

Effective communication is a skill you can develop and improve. As with the development of any skill, you must start with what you have. What you have is who you are, how you think, and how you interact with others. What you may need is a clear and accurate understanding of how you come across—in other words, self-awareness.

Businesses need associates that...

> *"...have a strong sense of self-awareness, who know how they come across, who exercise good self-control, who are empathetic and skilled at listening, resolving conflicts, and gaining cooperation."*
>
> —Daniel Goleman,
> *Emotional Intelligence*

Surprisingly, very few people have a clear and accurate understanding of how they come across to others. This is why executive coaching is such a big business and why complete and detailed feedback is so valuable. We long for others to tell us what we don't know. We want honesty from the people around us, yet all too often we create an environment in which others seldom offer honesty because we often resent the truth and it seldom leads to real change.

What Is It Like to Be on the Other Side of You?

> *"If you don't know how you are coming across to other people, you are the only one who doesn't know."*
>
> —Bill Wheless,
> founder, Wheless-Wyatt Communications

What is it like to talk to you?

- Do you listen intently with your ears, eyes, heart, and mind?

- Do you look the speaker in the eye or look around him or her to see if someone more interesting has entered the room?

- Do you show impatience by glancing at the clock, interrupting, or finishing the speaker's sentences to hurry him or her up?

- Do you focus, or do you allow distractions such as fidgeting or, God forbid, checking your e-mail or texting, when someone is talking to you, believing as so many people mistakenly do that you can successfully do two things at once and that it's only bad manners when someone other than you is doing it?

What *is* it like to talk to you?

What is it like to listen to you talk?

- Are you clear, focused, concise, and interesting?

- Do you ramble on and on, never getting to the point (assuming you actually have a point)?

- Do you enunciate clearly with enough volume to be heard? Or do you mumble or start and restart your sentences, thereby losing everyone's attention?

What *is* it like to listen to you talk?

How Do You Come Across?

Take a few minutes to consider the answers to the following questions. Be honest with yourself. Perhaps some of the questions will give you pause to think. In which ways can you improve?

Communication Self-Analysis

1. When you speak, do you add value to the conversation and have something worthwhile to say, or do you speak up just because everyone else is talking and you feel that you should talk too?

2. Do you speak from a position of knowledge and demonstrate that you are clearly prepared and have done your homework?

3. Are your remarks well organized, or does your listener wonder where you are going?

4. Do you speak using clear, everyday language, or do you bog down your message with business speak and words your audience won't understand? Are you clear and concise, or do you ramble on and on, never getting to the point?

5. Do you include only the information that will get you to the point, or do you muddy the message by trying to include everything you know, just so the listener will know you know?

6. Are you interesting? Do you include relevant stories and examples when you speak?

7. Do you have a clear point of view?

8. Do you express your thoughts clearly?

9. Can you make technical information understandable?

10. Do you start to talk before you know what you are going to say?

11. Do you speak too fast? Do you speak too slowly?

12. Do you enunciate clearly?

13. Do you consider how your listener may feel about your remarks and address any concerns *before* someone might bring them up?

14. Do you remain professional when a listener is argumentative?

15. Are the signals others receive from you the signals you intend to send?

16. Do people with whom you interact feel you are open or that you have a hidden agenda?

17. Are you aware of time and respect your listeners by projecting a sense of urgency?

18. Do your listeners feel safe when asking questions or challenging your point of view?

19. Do you listen more than you talk?

20. Do you focus on the speaker and listen intently until he or she is finished speaking, or do you consider what you will say when it is your turn to talk?

21. Do you resist the temptation to multitask when you are supposed to be listening?

22. Do you listen from the speaker's point of view and put yourself in his or her shoes so you can listen emphatically?

23. Do you work to "hear" what is *not* being said that may be important, in addition to what is being said?

24. Do you paraphrase the speaker's message in your own words for clarity and to avoid misunderstandings?

25. Do you seek to understand the speaker's position before imposing your own point of view?

26. Do people leave their interaction with you feeling heard and respected?

Now that you have considered these questions in light of how you see yourself, look back over the questions and consider how those with whom you interact on a day-to-day basis would answer these questions about you. Would the answers be the same as yours?

Wouldn't you want to know?

Wouldn't you want to know whether people feel you ramble, are disorganized, boring, or waste their time? Wouldn't you want to know whether people feel you are not listening or clearly disrespecting them and their point of view?

Self-awareness is the key to effective communication. Take the time to know yourself and learn how others perceive you. Address any behaviors that may get in the way of your being the best communicator you can be. The skills you use to be effective one-on-one are the same skills you will take with you when you step in front of an audience.

Part 2 - Developing Your Message

<<<<<<<<<<<<<<<<<<<<<<<<<<<<<<<<<<<<<<<<<<<<<<<<<<<<<<<<<<<<<<<<<<<<<<<<<<<<<<<

Getting Started

When you learn that you have a presentation to write and deliver, when should you start? The obvious answer is "right away." In reality, however, presenters often sit down with their computers the night before their presentation and begin by designing slides or finding slides they already have and making their remarks fit the slides. Or, even worse, on their way out the door, they have an assistant hand them a flash drive with a presentation already loaded, and their plan is to wade through the slides while the audience pretends to be engaged. Sound familiar?

Of course there is a better way. Is there an easier way? No, but there is a better way.

If you are going to break out of the packs of boring, ineffective presenters out there, you should never expect people to sit on the other side of you and listen to what you have to say if you haven't respected their time enough to ensure that what you have to say is of value to them.

There is no getting around it. Being an effective presenter is work. It is work, however, that shows you are a disciplined thinker, that you have something to say that will be of value to your audience, and that you respect them enough to put in the effort.

The minute you know you have a presentation to deliver, begin to think about it. How can you make it effective? How can you make it different?

Develop a Creative File

As you go through your day, you will experience people, stories, and situations. Some of these will catch your interest. Make notes. You don't have to know at that time how you will use the information.

Drop your notes into what Wheless-Wyatt Communications founder Bill Wheless calls a creative file. When you sit down to develop a presentation, look through your file for ideas, stories that will help you make a point, add humor, or make your presentation more interesting. You'll be amazed at how you can use your own life experiences to add flavor to your presentations.

Steps to Developing a Winning Presentation

Step 1: Learn about your audience

Step 2: Establish your goal

Step 3: Determine how to get there

Step 1: Learn About Your Audience

There are two sets of expectations—yours and those of your audience. Active learning and communication

Presenting is not about you. It's about the audience.

take place when there is an overlap between what the presenter wants to convey and what the audience wants to receive. There is no point wasting your time or that of your audience by presenting information they don't want to hear or already know.

Before you can plan an effective presentation, you must know about the people to whom you are speaking. Your remarks must take many things into consideration, including their ages and general knowledge of the subject. Most important, you must know *why it is in their interest to listen to you.* You know why you are speaking to them, but why should they listen to you?

Who Are They? What Are Their Ages, Genders, and Geographical and Cultural Representations?

Knowing the ages of those in your audience will keep you from making embarrassing and costly errors, as David did.

Oops!

When we began to talk about knowing your audience in one of our training sessions, David, one of the participants, shot up his hand and said, "Let me tell you what happened to me."

David told us that when he was a young financial consultant, trying to build his business, someone suggested he sponsor a free retirement seminar. Excited, he went to a local convention hotel, leased a room for his presentation, arranged for refreshments, and took care of all the details. He then took out a newspaper ad to announce his free seminar.

David worked and reworked and rehearsed his presentation until he felt great about it.

(story continues on next page)

(continued from previous page)

On the night of the seminar, he decided not to meet his audience in advance. Rather he asked a colleague to introduce him. David would come in from the back of the room with his head held high, moving with energy and purpose. That is what he did.

When he got about twenty feet into the room, he froze. We all asked him, "What was wrong?"

"What was wrong," he moaned, "is that I was looking out over an audience made up of people at least sixty years old."

"What was wrong with that?" we asked.

He explained, "My message was that if you want to live in retirement in the manner to which you will have become accustomed, you have to start planning *early*."

Knowledge of your audiences' ages will give you an idea of the things they may or may not have experienced during their lifetimes. For example, telling a story to make a point by referencing *The Tonight Show Starring Johnny Carson* probably will produce puzzled looks on the faces of those too young to remember the program. If you refer to modern technology that is very familiar to recent college graduates, you may lose the attention of older members of your audience who have no clue what you are talking about.

Gender is important for many reasons. You wouldn't speak to a group of women in the same manner as you would a group of men. Your relatable stories, analogies, and quotes might be entirely different. Also consider that, in general, women are motivated by feelings and men by facts.

Geographical considerations are important as well. You will want to know whether your audience has had to travel a long distance to be with you. With all the inconvenience that goes along with travel, delays could cause them to be late or to arrive dog tired. As the presenter you could prepare for this by adjusting your start time or keeping your audience energized with frequent breaks.

Knowing the geographical representation of your audience is also important because if you use slang and terms that are common to the area, some audience members may not know what you are talking about. You also may have some language barriers to overcome. In the past, audiences in New York were very different audiences from those in Atlanta. This isn't

> *"The mind can only absorb what the seat can endure."*
>
> —anonymous

as true anymore since people often end up working far from where they grew up. Almost any audience will be made up of people from across the country.

There are many reasons to consider geographical representation. For example making eye contact is considered disrespectful in some cultures. Know the culture and mores of the area in which you are speaking.

What Is Your Audience's General Education Level? What Are Their Jobs and Skill Levels?

Your job as a presenter is to connect with your audience. In order to do that without speaking over their heads or using highly technical terms they don't understand, you must learn as much as you can about their training and level of comprehension regarding your subject. Always assume someone in the audience won't understand you, and work to avoid that. The quickest way to insult an audience is to speak to them in a language they don't understand. It is your responsibility as a presenter to know your audience and deliver a message that is clear, concise, and understandable.

What Do They Already Know About Your Subject?

How do they feel about you, your company, and your point of view? Where are they likely to disagree with you? If you have reason to believe some members of your audience may have a negative view of your topic, this is the time to change their thinking. Unaddressed objections will remain deterrents to your goal. Ignoring them will keep the elephant wandering around the room, attracting attention rather than keeping the focus on your message.

Audiences will appreciate that you have considered their points of view and thought through why they should think differently and how it will benefit them to do so. If there is an objection you are fairly certain is in their minds, don't hope it won't come up. Bring it up yourself and discuss it.

What Level of Detail Do They Want? General or Very Specific?

Perhaps you have had your personality assessed by using the DISC profile. DISC is a group of psychological inventories developed by John Geier and others and based on the 1928 work of psychologist William Moulton Marston. The DISC profile basically concludes that we all fall predominately into one of four personality types. Knowing the personality types of your audience allows you to target your remarks and level of detail to your best advantage.

"D" (dominant) people are outgoing and task oriented. They are typically company presidents, CEOs, and strong leaders. They have enormous demands on their time and want you to "just spit it out." Don't tell them what they already know. When addressing these people, be brief and clear, and don't include unnecessary information.

"I" (influencing) people love to talk. They are outgoing and people oriented and are typically salespeople, trainers, and speakers. They don't want to hear a lot of detail. When addressing these people, get them involved. They love to participate.

"S" (steady) personality types are people oriented. They are sympathetic to others' needs and are usually counselors, teachers, nurses, or volunteers. When presenting to these types of people, let them know how they can help you.

"C" (cautious) types want all the detail. They are typically accountants, investigators, engineers, and auditors. When presenting to these people, bring all your background information such as statistics and charts.

You don't have to run personality tests on your audience. The positions they represent, their jobs, should give you a good idea of what their DISC designation would be, and you can plan your presentation from there. For example, an audience of nurses would reflect a general personality type of "S", while a group of accountants most likely would be predominantly "C" personalities.

Suppose you have a mixed audience. Suppose you have "D" personalities who only want the bottom line and also "C" personalities who want all the detail. If you speak to this audience using all the detail, you will lose the "D" personalities' attention, and you probably won't get their attention back. You should speak top level and let the audience know that all the detail is available if they have a question or want to know how you developed your position. You can have a handout of all of your supporting data to give out after your presentation. Speaking top level will keep the "C" personalities intrigued, particularly if they know the data is available for the asking.

How Many People Will Be in the Audience? How Will They Be Seated? Will They Be Eating? How Will They Be Dressed?

Logistically, your delivery to three people will be much different than if you have an audience of four hundred. In a smaller group you may be seated around a conference table. Handouts, instead of projected images, will be more appropriate (if you use visual aids at all). A larger audience may require sound amplification.

Seating is important. You'll want everyone in your audience to be able to see and hear you. Be careful that a lectern is not blocking the screen if you are projecting slides, or that your body is not blocking your projection screen. If you're presenting from a raised stage, consider how you will appear to the people who are sitting right in front of you. Ladies, this is not the time to wear a dress or skirt!

In smaller groups U-shape seating allows everyone to have eye contact with one another. This is particularly helpful in presentations in which there is audience participation.

Larger audiences may be seated either theater style or around tables. If round tables are used, see if space will allow the participants to be seated only around half of the table so they can see you without having to turn around in their seats.

Lunch or dinner meetings can be problematic for presenters. Whenever you can avoid having an audience eating while you are speaking, it will work not only to your advantage but also to your audience's advantage. We live in a multitasking age. Unfortunately we have never gotten better at doing more than one thing at a time, nor will we ever. Our brains are simply not wired to focus on more than one thing at a time and to do either well. Eating will be a distraction for the person eating and for the person sitting next to him or her.

Request to speak before or after the meal. Ask that the servers not clear away plates once you have begun your presentation. This may sound self-serving, but it isn't. Audience members will appreciate not having the distraction as much as you will, particularly if you're so engaging they can't bear to miss one word!

You should know how your audience will be dressed and use that information to your advantage. If you're addressing a group of plant workers, you'll look very much like an outsider if they're in denim and you're dressed like a senior executive. Dress to reflect the audience, but just a step above. Remember that you are always representing your organization and the image it intends to project.

How Do You Learn All This Information About Your Audience? Ask.

- You can say to the meeting planner, "Please tell me everything you can about my audience and the venue in which I will be presenting."

- You can talk with the head of the division you will be addressing. For example you might say, "I'll be presenting our plan to your division next week. How does your team feel about the changes? Where are they likely to disagree?"

- You can talk with the gatekeeper for your prospective client. For example you might say, "I'm meeting with Mr. Jones on Thursday. Does he like a lot of detail, or does he prefer a top-level overview?"

- You can say to your audience, "I'll be presenting our plan to you next week and asking for your approval. What information would you like to see included?"

It may seem like a lot of work to learn about your audience, but doing so is vital to your success as a presenter.

Step 2: Establish Your Goal

A True Story?

Albert Einstein was on a train from Hartford, Connecticut. The conductor was passing through the railcar, taking passengers' tickets. When he got to Dr. Einstein, Dr. Einstein looked in his upper coat pocket. He looked in his lower coat pockets. As he opened his coat, still looking for his ticket, it was apparent that he was becoming upset. "Please, sir," said the conductor. "I know who you are. I am quite certain you bought a ticket." The conductor passed on by, taking up tickets from the other passengers.

When he reached the end of the railcar, he turned and saw to his horror that Dr. Einstein was crawling around on the floor beneath his seat. Rushing up to him, the conductor took Dr. Einstein by the elbow, and helping him up, said, "Please, sir! As I said, I know who you are!"

"I know who I am too," said Dr. Einstein. "What I don't know is where I am going!"

Too often presenters sit down at their computers and start typing away. They have no idea where they're going with their message. Maybe they'll figure that out somewhere along the way—or maybe not.

Clients with whom I work hear me ask this over and over again, "What is your goal?"

Stephen R. Covey, author of the bestselling book *The 7 Habits of Highly Effective People*, said it so well with his second habit, **"Begin with the end in mind."** You must know where you are going before you start to think about how you will get there.

What do you want your presentation to accomplish? If you are successful, what will have happened? When you establish a goal—and you should clearly state it in one sentence—you can then begin to put words on paper. You can then create a logical flow to your information that will bring your audience to exactly the place you want them to be.

Having a goal is a way to focus your thoughts and refrain from including too much information that muddies your message. If what you're considering including gets you to your goal, include it. If not, leave it out.

A goal is rarely "to tell," such as "I just want to tell them about the project." A goal would be "I want to tell them about the project so they will approve it." Another goal might be "I want to tell them about the project and hear any objections before we go any further." A goal should include an action to be taken.

You will be amazed at how establishing a goal will clarify your work and make developing a presentation easier. You should establish a goal in all types of communication in which you engage. Before you write an e-mail, ask yourself, "What is the purpose of this e-mail, and what do I want the recipient to do after having read it?" Before calling a meeting or scheduling a conference call, ask yourself, "What do I want this meeting or call to accomplish?" You can then plan who should be there and other specifics based on your goal.

Having a goal before you ever open your mouth or write a single word requires that you have disciplined thoughts. Having a goal will keep you focused, allow for conciseness and clarity, and contribute to the effectiveness of your communication.

Step 3: Determine How to Get There

What's Up?   So What?   Now What?

Structure and Organization:
What to Include and Where to Include It

Every presentation should have three parts:
        1. The Open: What's Up?
        2. The Middle: So What?
        3. The Close: Now What?

The most important parts are the open and the close. Why? The open tells your audience why they should listen, and the close tells them what they should do as a result of having heard what you said.

The Open: What's Up?

In the open you should do three things:
1. Engage the audience.
2. Tell them your purpose.
3. Tell them what you are going to do.

Engaging an Audience

Everyone in every audience, everywhere, asks the same question, "What is in this for me?" The sooner you answer that question for your audience, the greater your chances are of being heard.

Engaging the audience means "grabbing" them, having them sit up and listen, and having them eager to hear what you have to say. Engaging your audience should be your first priority. Too often we hear boring, predictable opens such as, "Good morning. My name is John Smith, and I'm from the southeast division. I've been asked to come today and share with you a little bit about the changes we're planning in the shipping department...blah, blah, blah."

Here's an open that engages the audience: "Good morning. What I'm about to tell you will affect each one of you and change the way you do your business. So please listen carefully, ask any questions you may have, and be ready to implement these changes before the end of the day. My name is John Smith, and I'm from the southeast division. What I'm going to tell you today is..."

How to Engage an Audience

- **Use a direct or startling statement**

You can use a direct or startling statement such as the one outlined above. Here are some other examples:

1. "Good morning. Today I'm going to tell you something you couldn't possibly already know."
2. "We have discovered some serious issues with your audit."
3. "I have some great news."

- **Ask a question**

Make sure the question is relevant to what you are going to talk about. When you engage the audience by asking a question, tell them what you want them to do. For example, you might say, "Think about how you would answer this question" or "Let me see a show of hands."

Here are some examples of opening questions:

1. "Have you ever made an assumption that was totally wrong?"
2. "If you had only one professional development opportunity this year, consider for a minute what you would choose."
3. "Please let me see a show of hands from those who would like to comment on the departmental changes we have suggested. Today we are going to hear from you."

Refrain from asking an obvious question. There is nothing more boring or predictable than being asked "How many of you would like to win a million dollars?"

- **Use a relevant quotation then pause**

   The quotation should relate to the subject of your presentation.

1. "There is an old Chinese proverb, 'The palest ink is stronger than the strongest memory.' **(pause)** Today we will learn some note-taking strategies that will help us..."
2. "Houston, we have a problem. **(pause)** The same could be said for us sitting here in Woonsocket, Rhode Island."
3. "Seek first to understand and then to be understood." **(pause)** I wonder if Stephen Covey coined that phrase for our benefit in the accounting department where we seem to do nothing but argue."

- **Make a prediction**

1. "I believe we will be out of business in six months."
2. "I think we will surpass our new business goal at the end of the year. That means we have some things to decide."
3. "I predict another merger within the next year."

- **Use props (real or imagined)**

Whoever said, "A picture is worth a thousand words" sure had the right idea. Audiences love to have something to look at (instead of wordy, confusing PowerPoint slides).

An audience would certainly be on the edges of their seats, totally engaged, wondering what is coming up if the presenter walked out with a baseball bat on his shoulder, or an axe in his hand, or a chicken on a leash (you get the idea).

Be aware, however, that if you pass your prop around, the audience will not listen to what you are saying. The person holding the prop will be distracted, and so will the people around him or her.

Props, used to engage an audience, can be very simple, even imaginary, as John shows us in the following story.

An Engaging Prop

When it was John's turn to present, he rose from his chair without saying a word. He walked to the center of the room, where the audience was seated at tables in a U shape. Still silent, he began to "draw" with his toe on the carpet. After a minute or so, he said, "I am drawing three imaginary boxes on the floor." He continued to "draw." "Because," he said, "I want to explain to you what it is like to be a stockbroker." John positioned himself in his first "box." "In my first box, I must prospect for business," he explained.

John then moved to his second "box." "In my second box, I must be a salesperson because I must make a client out of the prospect I discovered in box number one." He then added the details.

Finally he stepped into his third "box." "Now," he said, "I am in customer service. Because I must take good care of the client I discovered in box number one and sold in box number two."

John's opening not only engaged the audience with an imaginary prop, but also left a visual image in the audiences' minds of exactly what is involved in being a stockbroker.

After engaging the audience, do two more things in your open. In addition to wanting to know what's in it for them, audiences want to know what to expect. So, in your open, you should tell them your purpose and tell them what you are going to do.

Here are examples of opens that engage, tell the purpose, and tell what the presenter is going to do:

1. "Ladies and gentlemen, we have a problem. My purpose in calling you together is to get this problem solved. I'm going to tell you what the problem is and why I think it came about, and then I'm going to ask for your ideas about how we should move ahead."
2. "Good morning. We could be saving thirty percent on advertising costs. I'm going to explain how and ask you to approve the plan I'm proposing."
3. "We're not having enough fun around here. I have three ideas I want to present and then get your thoughts on which you would like to pursue. The first thing I have in mind is..."

The Middle: So What?

The middle of your presentation is where you put your "stuff"—your main points and supporting data. Be careful, however, that the middle doesn't become a long-running narrative in which the middle turns to muddle, or you will lose your audience's attention.

Organizing Your Thoughts

Your presentation should be logically laid out. The audience should not have to wonder where you are going. They will not work to stay with you. Your points should be easy for your audience to follow. The information should flow logically from one point to the next.

Having your presentation logically crafted not only will help your audience stay on track but also will help you, the presenter, as well.

Here are some ideas to organize the middle of your presentation so that it flows logically:

- **Points**

If you use points, tell your audience in advance how many points you have. For example you might say, "I have three points I want to make today." Otherwise they will wonder when you are on point number two how many more points you have. If you have more than four or five points, you may want to rethink your presentation. There is a limit to the adult attention span. If it is absolutely necessary to have six or seven points, determine how you can "chunk" them into three- and four-point segments. For example you might say, "My first three points concern our production timetable, and my last four points explain how the timetable affects shipping." The human brain is better able to remember three- and four-point "chunks." It is no accident that telephone numbers are divided into "chunks," as are Social Security and credit card numbers.

At the end of each point, reiterate where you are. For example you might say, "That was my first point. The second point I want to make is..."

- **Time**

"I want to tell you what happened in the past, where we are now, and what to expect in the future."

- **Topics/issues**

"If we are to be successful, we need to focus our attention on four issues."

- **Problem, analysis, solution**

"We have a problem. I'm going to explain what the problem is, what I believe has caused it, and the solution I'm proposing."

However you decide to organize your presentation, remember that you are leading your audience to your goal.

> The best presentations are the ones that make sense.

The Close: Now What?
Directing Your Audience

The close is the second most important part of your presentation; the engaging opening is the first. The close is critical because these will be the last words your audience hears from you (you should take questions *before* the close), and you want them walking out with your most important points firmly in their minds. The close is also important because in the close you'll tell the audience what they should think or do as a result of having heard your remarks.

In a strong close you will do two things: **summarize** your main points and **direct** the audience what you want them to do. Here are some examples:

1. "In closing let me summarize that we must address the problem now. We must pull employees from every department to work on the issue, and we must reevaluate in thirty days. Please let me know by the end of the day which employees you wish to assign to the task."

2. "Let me close by saying once again that we have all worked very hard. We've exceeded our goal by twenty percent. We've created new, better processes as a result. In recognition, please give your teams a Friday of their choice off between now and the end of the year."

Developing Your Notes

Working without notes is not impressive; it's dangerous. It's much better to have notes and not need them than to need them and not have them. Notes serve as an outline to keep you on track. There is no need to hide the fact that you have notes; staying on track is a consideration to your audience. Even so, you don't want your notes to be a distraction.

You will come across as more comfortable and conversational if you develop your notes in short bullet points that will remind you of what you want to say. Make sure the font is large enough to be easily read, and by all means, number your cards or pages in case you drop them and they end up out of order.

Organize your notes according to your own preference, and don't include more information than you need. Practice will help you know what to include and what to leave out.

If you must write out everything you're going to say in script form, be sure to write in the manner in which you speak. We don't talk in long, drawn out sentences. In fact often we speak in incomplete sentences. Practice until you can speak without staying glued to your notes. If you write out your entire message, be aware of the problems associated with this type of delivery. For example if someone interrupts to ask a question that you plan to cover on page ten and you're only on page four, it will be difficult to recover from that. Bulleted notes will give you more flexibility.

Did I Really Do That? Say It Isn't So

Reciting your message—as opposed to connecting your message to your audience—has a predictable outcome.

An executive on his way to deliver a speech to a large audience grabbed his script on the way out the door. Although he had every word he was going to say printed before him, he planned to rely on the teleprompter.

All went well, or so he thought.

In the limo on the way back to his hotel, he noticed that page thirty-seven was in his script twice. And that is exactly how he recited it, just as it was loaded into the teleprompter from the script he had supplied.

He hadn't realized it. No problem; neither had the audience.

Visual Aids

Once you have completed the draft of your presentation, it's time to go back and consider whether visuals will *aid the audience* and help you reach your goal.

Well designed, professionally handled visual aids can make your message easier to understand, more convincing, more credible, and more interesting. Unfortunately, too often, visuals are not well designed or professionally handled. It is common for the presenter's back to be to the audience as he or she reads one poor visual after another.

Visual aids can either aid your presentation or destroy it. The biggest problems exist with the use, or misuse, of PowerPoint presentations, handouts, and decks (sales presentations walked through page by page as a disinterested client pretends to listen). Let's begin with the biggest problem of all, PowerPoint presentations.

PowerPoint

Where PowerPoint is concerned, you probably already know there is a problem. You may not be able, however, to put your finger on just what the problem is. When I point it out, it may surprise you.

What I am going to explain to you is the greatest obstacle to effective communication I see. I see this same issue in all areas of the country, in all industries, and at all levels, from entry-level employees to chief executive officers and chairmen of the board. Unfortunately this problem is only getting worse.

To understand the problem, you must forget your title. We are all in sales. That title isn't limited to those who bring in clients and customers. We are *all* in sales. As we go through our day, we constantly sell our ideas to others and encourage them to buy in and to commit their talents and energies to go in our direction.

If we are all in sales, we want people to do business with us, to want to partner with us, and to want to commit. We want our internal customers, our teams, and our colleagues to do business with us. We want people outside our organizations, our external customers, to do business with us.

We all do business with people we like and trust. That's where the problem lies.

Ninety-three percent of our believability comes from what people observe about us visually—our appearance, demeanor, confidence, and eye contact, and what they hear in our voice (conviction, energy, or authority, for example).

When our slides or handouts become our presentation, we give away our power. Too many presenters spend more time designing their visuals, slides, handouts, and decks than considering how they will connect with their audience. Consequently the presenters, the people we want our audience to do business with, slip into the background.

We give away our power by focusing our audience's attention away from us and toward PowerPoint screens, handouts, and decks. We demote ourselves to the position of slide narrators, and even then no one is listening, because they are trying to read the mass of information on the screen, or they are pretending to try while they take the opportunity to think of something else entirely.

We lose any connection with our listeners when their eyes focus on our materials and not on us.

A Relevant Story

Throughout all of our years working with clients, we have particularly enjoyed receiving articles, stories, and experiences from our clients that affirm something we have taught.

Several years ago, a client sent us a copy of an article that appeared in *Sales Life* magazine. The article, "An Electrifying Presentation," was written by John O'Toole, who was the chief executive officer of the American Association of Advertising Agencies in New York and the former chairman of Foote, Cone & Belding Communications.

Mr. O'Toole told of an experience in which he and his team were pitching a prospective client for their business. They were one of several agencies making presentations that day in hopes of landing a new client. When it came time for Mr. O'Toole and his team to present, the power failed and all the electricity went out in the building. The client, eager to make a decision, would not allow any presentations to be rescheduled.

Without their visuals, Mr. O'Toole and his team focused on the clients and had their attention in return. They were able to really connect with their audience.

The outcome was that Mr. O'Toole's team won the business over competitors who had enjoyed unlimited electricity. He stated that he has been conscious since that day of how much we give away when our audience focuses on our materials and not on us, the people who must make the charts and exhibits believable.

> *"Selling is accomplished by one individual persuading another. Anything that intrudes between the two parties during that process must either contribute to the persuasion, or it will surely detract from it."*
>
> – John O'Toole,
> *Sales Life*, October 1993

Think about the last presenter who really affected you, the one who just nailed it for you. Most likely that presenter used few, if any, visuals.

The most memorable presenters rely on their delivery style, rather than a slide deck, to make their points. They begin by having a goal, by knowing exactly what they want their message to achieve.

Then they include only the information that will help them reach their goal.

> There are some things technology hasn't improved.

PowerPoint has become a staple of modern-day presentations. In fact you could say the only thing that has risen as quickly as the adoption of PowerPoint is the increased boredom and wasted time experienced when it is used incorrectly (which is most of the time).

We have all experienced it—the feeling of dread as the light fades and a PowerPoint slide appears, the first of many with a bunch of statistics and other "stuff" that we have no interest in or that has nothing to do with what the presenter wants to achieve.

That may be because the presenter has no idea what the point of the presentation is, or what he or she wants us to do as a result of hearing his or her remarks. The presenter proceeds to waste our time by reading all that "stuff" to us. Instead of gathering us all together, why didn't he or she just send us the slides and let us read them ourselves? (Unfortunately too often a "presenter" reads every word he or she says off a PowerPoint slide anyway.)

We are the victims of so many presentations that are one badly designed slide after another. Yet many presenters continue to present in this same way over and over. How can such a great presentation tool go so horribly wrong?

PowerPoint is not the problem; the people who use it incorrectly are. It somehow seems to escape attention that the *presenter* is the one who delivers the message (or fails to in many cases).

The Problem

Since I see this so often, and I see it getting worse all the time, I've done a lot of thinking about why this is happening. I think there are two reasons.

The first reason I think this occurs is because many presenters think this is the way they are *supposed* to present because that is what they see other presenters doing. The second reason may be a bit harder to swallow, particularly if it applies to you. Too many presenters use PowerPoint as a crutch for their own lack of skill, knowledge, or preparation. They invest too much time in creating slides rather than thinking through and planning their message. They simply fire up the software and start banging away, or they have someone else hand them a stack of slides, and they make their remarks fit what is on the slides, regardless of what their goal is.

> PowerPoint should be used to aid the *audience* not the presenter.

What about you? If this doesn't apply to you, it doesn't apply. If it sounds familiar, this is your opportunity to acknowledge the problem and fix it.

In my presentation skills training classes, participants deliver their prepared presentations to have their content and delivery style critiqued by me and to receive feedback from their peers.

If someone gives a presentation and uses slides that are much too busy or otherwise incorrectly designed, or if they have a PowerPoint slide up the entire time they are talking, once they have concluded their presentation, I often ask them to deliver their presentation again without the slides.

If I see all the blood drain out of their faces, I'll quickly add, "Okay, you can use your slides as your notes, but don't project them. I don't want us to see them."

The other presenters, who serve as the audience, have no idea why I am doing what I am doing because we haven't talked about any of this yet. When the second presentation is over, the one without the audience seeing the visuals, before I say a word, 100 percent of the time someone will say something like, "Wow, the second time was so much better. I really understood what he was talking about. When he used the slides, I was lost." The others quickly join in and express the same feeling.

Now why do you suppose that is? It is because when the presenter talks at the same time that he is expecting his audience to read a slide or digest what is on it, or look at a handout, the audience has no choice but to divide their attention.

> **"To do two things at once is to do neither."**
>
> —Publilius Syrus,
> Latin writer

We cannot do two things at once. We can't read a PowerPoint slide and comprehend what we are reading while we are trying to listen to the presenter. There is little chance our eyes will be at the same place the presenter is referencing, unless, of course, the slide is properly designed with one idea per slide, which unfortunately is rarely the case.

Nor can we comprehend what a presenter is saying or what is covered in a meeting while we are checking our e-mail or texting. As much as we'd like to think we can, we can't do two things at once. There is no way to come away with a clear understanding.

Too often we walk out of a meeting with no idea of what was decided or who is to do what. Overwhelming PowerPoint slides and a presenter who talks over them often are responsible for that. It's no wonder we get all mixed up. We simply cannot concentrate on two things at once.

PowerPoint can be a powerful tool, and I use it often. Just like any tool, however, it must be used as it was intended—to *aid* the presentation, not *be* the presentation.

When to Use PowerPoint

The first step in learning to use PowerPoint correctly is to know if and when it should be used.

The decision to use visual aids should be your *last* step in developing any presentation. You will have developed your theme, goal, and main points with supporting data. You will have segmented your information into a strong open that engages your audience and tells them your purpose and what you are going to do; a middle that logically presents your main points; and a summarizing and directive close. Now is the time to go back and consider whether you should use visuals to clarify, add interest, or otherwise aid your audience. I can't say this too often: **Visuals should be used to benefit the audience, not the presenter.** If you are in doubt, leave them out.

If you decide to use visuals, (PowerPoint, hand-outs, or decks), they should *complement* what you say, add to it, and make it stronger. They should not *be* what you say.

Sometimes clients will say that their bosses expect and require PowerPoint slides. They are told that if they don't have PowerPoint, they don't have a presentation and that it appears they took no time to prepare if they don't have slides. A boss who would make such a remark has no concept of effective communication and how much more effort it takes to present from a position of knowledge and skill rather than rely on slides. I tell my clients, "You have to keep your job. Satisfy your boss. Use PowerPoint. Just learn to use it well."

Designing Your Slides

If you have made the determination that visuals will aid your presentation, you'll need to know how to effectively design your slides. **Remember, slides should be created for the benefit of the audience and not for the presenter.**

The Billboard Rule

Each slide should have one clear, easily understood point. It should adhere to what I call the Billboard Rule. If I can drive by your slide at seventy miles per hour and get the main point of the slide, it's a good slide; if not, it's too busy.

The 1-6-1-6 Principle

Seeing what was happening with PowerPoint, such as entire presentations projected word for word on the screen, a solution began to bounce around. I have yet to discover its origin, but I believe it is an effective answer to the problem.

- Limit your visual to **1** concept

- Limit the body copy to **6** lines

- Limit each bullet/point to **1** line

- Limit each line to **6** words

Let's look at some examples of the 1-6-1-6 Principle. First is a slide with the 1-6-1-6 Principle **ignored**.

My guess is that this slide is fairly representative of slides you've seen in meeting after meeting. How can the audience possibly digest what is on the screen and listen to the presenter at the same time?

FY 2013 Budget Process

- Next year's budget will reflect a 5 percent decrease in overall expenditures as compared to 2012. The following guidelines should be used in preparing your departmental budgets.

- Capital budget requests must be reviewed by the budget review committee no later than August 30. All requests received after that date will be denied.

- Operating increases in excess of 3 percent over FY 12 must be approved by the division vice president. (All requests to the DVP must be submitted on form 934 by August 1.)

- New hires must be submitted on the new hire requisition form and will require an appearance before the budget review committee. (It is expected that some layoffs will be necessary in order to reach our 5 percent cutback.)

- There will be no increases approved in travel and entertainment. T&E budgets for 2013 will be reviewed very carefully.

- As a matter of fact, don't bother to submit a budget at all. The budget committee will do it for you.

Source: Bill Wheless's "Communicating
Successfully in Business" workshop

Below is the same information with the 1-6-1-6 Principle **observed**.

FY 2013 Budget Process

- 5 percent decrease overall
- Capital budgets by Aug 30
- Operating over 3 percent requires DVP approval
- Justify new hires before the budget committee
- No increase in T&E
- Don't bother; we'll do it for you

Source: Bill Wheless's "Communicating Successfully in Business" workshop

---

This second example is so much clearer. These bullet points will be effective if the presenter projects them one at a time as he or she references them and adds detail.

The slide below is typical of so many PowerPoint slides we see. To protect the identity of the company and presenter, all of the figures have been changed. I tell you that in case you actually take the time to check the calculations—because they won't add up!

Selected Growth Trends

($ in Millions)

	2007	2008	2009	2010	2011
Average Costs	46,338	51,788	37,590	68,749	70,044
Average Revenues	43,190	45,496	44,909	47,001	49,472
Net Interest Income	2,660	2,585	2,929	3,145	3,108
Other Income	1,146	1,329	1,654	1,626	1,774
Net Income	859	976	978	327	1,294

Source: Bill Wheless's "Communicating Successfully in Business" workshop

The presenter was referencing two years of revenue figures, 2010 and 2011. If he wanted to reference only two years, why is all the other information on the slide?

Look at the same information shown in a visual image below.

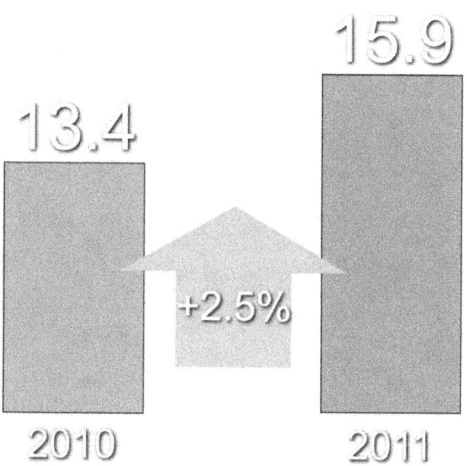

Source: Bill Wheless's "Communicating Successfully in Business" workshop

A study performed by the University of Minnesota and 3M found that presentations with visual support are 43 percent more persuasive than those that do not include visual elements. Visual support helps listeners understand abstract concepts. Complex data can be organized and reduced to a graphic, chart, or table to make a point clearly and concisely. Effective visual support maintains listener interest and increases retention of the material being presented. You may hear the argument that someone is a visual learner and that they need PowerPoint in order to retain the information. Note, however, that visual support means *visual images,* not paragraph after paragraph of words or column after column of numbers on a page.

The BECS Principle

When designing slides, in addition to following the 1-6-1-6 Principle, consider what I call the BECS Principle. That's an acronym. People in business love acronyms. In some industries, I believe if we took all the acronyms away, they would have to close their doors. In fact there is a name for using lots of acronyms: Severe Acronym Overload Disorder. You may prefer to see it like this: SAOD. Okay, back to the BECS principle.

B: Balance Your Slides Visually

In the English language, we read from top to bottom and from left to right. Each slide should be titled at the top and clearly describe the point of the slide. You should arrange the information so the eye follows easily from top to bottom and from left to right. Use arrows and other visual cues to help guide your audience through the visual.

E: Evaluate

Evaluate your slides from the audience's perspective. Is the visual easy to absorb within five to eight seconds? Is it clear where the eye should travel and where the audience should look first? Does the visual hold the attention of your audience and support a key point in your message?

C: Color

Color attracts attention and increases people's willingness to pay attention to your visuals, but color should not overpower the message. Colors should stay consistent throughout the presentation, as should the design of your slides.

S: Simplicity

Simplicity in presentation slides allows your message to get through. Remember, less is more.

That's Beautiful!

Your slides or handout pages should get the attention you intend them to get, which is to clarify a point or to add interest for your audience. They should not evoke comments and thoughts such as, "That's beautiful!" or "How in the world did she figure out how to design that slide?"

Your slide design should not be the focus of the slide or even attract attention. The slide should help your audience stay on point. Good communication is, after all, about connecting your message to the audience and not about who has the coolest slides.

Title Slides and Others

Title slides are often included as the first slide in a presentation. A title slide can include the name of the presentation, the presenter, the date, and often has the company logo. When deciding whether or not to use a title slide, consider if it adds anything to your presentation. Is there a good reason to project something that has already been said or will be said? Title slides can take the attention of your audience away from you at that critical time when you must engage them and get them listening.

The same advice goes for closing slides that simply say "Thank You" or something similar. Why should you include a closing slide if it takes the focus away from you?

In light of what we have said about slides and their purpose, is there ever a good reason to have a slide with a question mark on it or a clip art character scratching his head when you are taking questions from the audience?

No matter how simple your slide is, it gives your audience an opportunity to avert their eyes, look at the screen, and think about something other than your presentation. Try as you may, the chances are that you won't get their attention back.

Handouts

People forget approximately 90 percent of everything that is said to them within twenty-four hours— not just spouses and children but *all* people. We don't actually forget; we just shift the information from our short-term memory to long-term memory. A handout is a good way to jog someone's memory.

Handouts typically contain more information than what you want to cover in your presentation. They may contain facts that support what you have to say or information that goes deeper than what you want to say but helps lead your audience to your same conclusions. The best handouts seize the opportunity to communicate additional information. Be careful, however, to include only information that your audience will find interesting and want to know. Don't pad your handouts with marginally relevant materials just to create a fat packet. Audiences are already overloaded with information. They want someone (and that is you) to sift through it and tell them what's important. If a one-page handout will do the job, don't feel you have to provide more.

Your handouts are an extension of your presentation, and you should prepare them with just as much care. Do you really have your audience in mind if, in order to have a handout, you just copy your PowerPoint slides? Take care that the pages are neat and easy to read and contain no typos. Handouts are a reflection of you and of your company. If they look like trash, they soon will be.

Audiences appreciate handouts; some audiences feel cheated if they don't get one. If they take notes on them, they feel a sense of personal investment in the material. People use well-designed handouts as a review tool long after your presentation has ended. As with any visual aid, use a handout if it will support your key points and provide additional information that will help you achieve your goal; if it won't, lose it.

Easel and Pad

Using an easel and pad is a great way to keep your audience with you as you develop ideas. These tools are low tech and easy to operate. Of course they are best used with smaller groups where everyone can easily see them. Avoid using an easel and pad if you can't write legibly or spell well.

Props

Props are a great way to create interest and engage an audience. Props give an audience a memorable picture that will stay in their minds much longer and more accurately than statistics, words, and other information that requires them to create their own images.

Props can be simple (such as the invisible boxes John used in the story mentioned earlier in the book) or more elaborate. Remember, your prop should *aid* your presentation not divert your audience's attention from you. If your prop is an elephant that you have brought into the room, you can bet your audience will not remember one word you say.

Memorable Presentations Using Props

The Lady and the Crisco

I'll never forget the luncheon I attended in which the guest speaker was a trim, fit woman in her mid-fifties. She spoke of her years of struggle to control her weight. She had gained and lost hundreds of pounds over the years.

One of her strategies, she said, was to control her sweet tooth by eating one Oreo cookie every day at four p.m.

"The problem with that," she said, as she reached under the lectern, took out an open can of Crisco, and scooped her hand into it to come out with a big, white blob of shortening "was that, within a month, I had added this much fat to my body."

If she had said the problem was that she had added 210 grams of fat, I never would have remembered the presentation. Because she used a memorable prop, however, I will never forget the lady and the Crisco.

The Best Pallet

There was a young man in one of my training sessions who was a sales representative for a manufacturing company. He delivered a presentation to sell a new pallet his company had designed.

Instead of throwing PowerPoint slides up to list the features of the pallet, he brought a pallet with him.

When he spoke of its light weight, he lifted it with one hand for all to see. When he spoke of its strength, he jumped up and down on it.

This young man knew how to use the power of a visual to create an impression. He probably sells lots of pallets.

The Creative Banker

One of my clients, a banker, told a story during a presentation skills training class. The story took place between 2008 and 2009, when the financial crisis was rearing its ugly head.

He was the second of three bankers asked to each address the annual meeting of the bank's stockholders with a presentation about what to expect in the next few months. Several hundred people were in the audience.

The first banker walked onto the stage where he had placed a column about three feet tall. On top of the column, under a black cloth, was a large, glass ball. The banker wore a headdress like a fortune-teller. He opened by saying the purpose of his presentation was to tell the stockholders what was going to happen. "Well," he said, as he whipped the black cloth off the crystal ball, "I'd have to be a fortune-teller to know for sure what's going to happen. What I can do is tell you what I *think* is going to happen."

He then went into his presentation, relayed his thoughts, used his collaborating material, and left the audience with an engaging, memorable presentation.

My client, who had to present next, just wanted to go home.

Beyond Visuals

Visuals that are well designed and used appropriately will not make up for a presenter's lack of skill. It is still the presenter who must connect with the audience and engage them, because it is the presenter who is the presentation, not the materials. To do that, you must learn how *you*, as the presenter, are coming across and if necessary work on your delivery skills.

If you follow the guidelines for using visuals effectively and work on your delivery, you can delight your audiences because you will be in the minority. That will be a wonderful surprise. You will be a presenter who actually communicates in a manner that adds value to the audience and reaches a goal—an experience in which no one's time is wasted (what a money saver!).

What It All Means

From time to time, probably almost every day, you are an audience member. As an audience member, you are probably rejoicing from what you have read so far in this book. If all presenters made the effort, we could reduce the number of information-packed presentations that leave audiences feeling numb and having no idea what they are supposed to take away from a meeting as a result of the time they have just spent **pretending to listen.**

As a presenter, though, you may have different feelings, because this means that in order to be an effective communicator, you must develop your skills. You must:

- learn about your audience

- spend time getting prepared

- develop a well thought-out goal

- weigh everything you will say or show against your goal

All of this takes motivation and work. Is it worth it to be different, to be unpredictable? If you believe every presentation is an opportunity for you to leave an impression, there is only one answer.

Part 3 - Delivering Your Message

<><><><><><><><><><><><><><><><><><><><><><><><><><><><><><><><><><><><><><><><><><><>

More Than the Words

You may have a great message, logically laid out, using just the right words, phrases, ideas, and thoughts. Even so, you will fail miserably when you step in front of an audience if you don't give the human element of communication the attention it requires.

> Words can be powerful, but the value we place on them is based on our impression of the person who says them.

Communication involves much more than the words you say. You communicate whenever you are **observed** or **heard**. Your demeanor and actions create the impression you make on others and the value they give to what you say. You constantly send signals that create those impressions.

Be aware that even before you begin your presentation, you are being sized up. How do you come across?

- Do you appear confident? Do you stand tall, with shoulders squared and head held high, and make eye contact with those around you?

- Are you relaxed? Smiling?

- Are you appropriately dressed?

- Do you carry yourself with authority?

- Do you look like you have something important to say?

- Do you move with energy and purpose?

Think about your own behavior when it comes to forming an opinion. Don't you make assumptions about people when you first observe them? It's natural to do so; they are sending signals—and so are you, as long as you can be observed or heard.

It's important to know the following:

You are always presenting.

A presentation is not solely defined as an activity in which you deliver information to an audience. A presentation is any contact you have with another person or persons. Your life is made up of a series of presentations. In each instance you have the opportunity to determine the outcome.

While it is important, of course, to prepare the content of your message so it addresses the needs of the audience and accomplishes your goal, never lose sight of the fact that your presentation begins long before you begin to speak.

The Three V's of Communication

If you want to be believable as you deliver your message, consider the work done by UCLA behavioral scientist Albert Mehrabian, considered by many to be the definitive researcher regarding communication. In his book, *Silent Messages: Implicit Communication of Emotions and Attitudes*, Dr. Mehrabian concludes that communication involves three elements: visual, vocal and verbal.

Visual - anything you can see in the presenter, including dress, body language, facial expression, eye contact, and posture.

Vocal - the sound of the presenter's voice, whether it is strong or weak, decisive or indecisive, monotone or energetic, etc.

Verbal - the actual words that are said.

Dr. Mehrabian concludes that these three elements—visual, vocal, and verbal—contribute to a presenter's **believability,** but they don't contribute equally. Here is the breakdown.

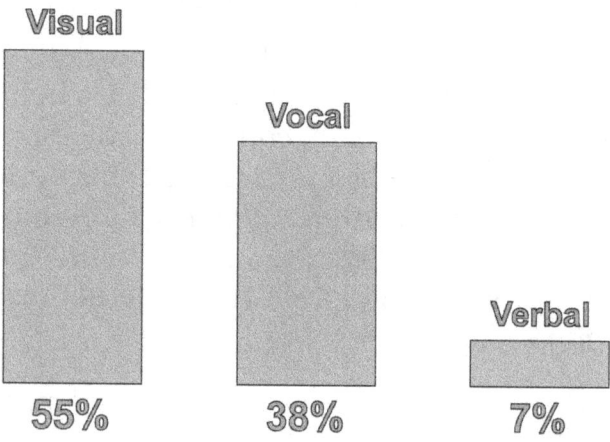

Ninety-three percent of your believability as a communicator comes from what others observe about you visually and from what they hear in your voice. Ninety-three percent!

You can probably think of instances in which your own beliefs support this theory. Perhaps there was a time when someone told that you he or she wasn't angry. The words might have been "I am not angry." But the tone of the person's voice and facial expression sent a different message.

> It's not what you say. It's how you say it.

When Dr. Martin Luther King delivered his famous "I Have a Dream Speech" on August 28, 1963, his words were powerful. They were made that way, however, by the passion on Dr. King's face and the conviction in his voice. His *delivery* is what makes us remember his famous words all these years later. Would his speech have such a place in history if he had delivered it simply by the written word? I doubt it.

If you want people to believe what you are saying, they first have to believe *you.* If you want to convince them, let them see your passion and hear your conviction. Make your words ring true.

Characteristics of Effective Presenters

Consider the traits in a presenter that you find positive, the characteristics that make you sit up and listen. Is there any reason why you can't exhibit the same characteristics?

Often when I ask my clients to describe the presenters they enjoy the most, their descriptions include the words listed below. As you reflect on these words—and any you would like to add—consider how they apply to you. You may want to include a checklist of these characteristics to refer to as you prepare and rehearse your presentations. How do you come across?

Approachable	Confident	Honest
Believable	Convincing	Knowledgeable
Charismatic	Creative	Passionate
Clear	Interesting	Personable
Concise	Energetic	Relatable
Comfortable	Engaging	Prepared

Listed on paper, these are just words. What is it, exactly, that we observe in a presenter that makes us attribute these characteristics? Let's define these words further.

Approachable

An approachable person smiles often and is relaxed and easy to be around. Audience members are not afraid to ask questions or make comments because the speaker's demeanor is welcoming.

Believable

Remember that 93 percent of a speaker's believability comes from what we observe about him visually and what we hear in his voice. We believe a speaker when it appears that he is prepared, has done his homework, and trusts what he is saying. His credibility is never in question because he has the confidence to say, "I don't know."

Charismatic

People gravitate toward people they describe as "charismatic." Charismatic people show a genuine interest in the people around them. They look you directly in the eye, ask questions about you, and keep their attention on you while you are talking. When you walk away, you feel good about the interaction. Charismatic speakers show a genuine interest in their audience. As an audience member, you can feel it.

Clear and Concise

All too often speakers obfuscate their messages by using words that no one understands. They say "obfuscate" instead of "confuse." They use business-speak (B.S.) words in an effort to sound smarter than they are or to try to hide the fact that they have nothing worthwhile to say. The audience sits there pretending to understand, but nothing close to communication is taking place. The low road to impressing an audience is to make them feel inferior by using words they won't understand.

An accomplished presenter says what needs to be said in as few words as possible and uses clear, everyday language. It's not about using big words; it's about using the right words.

> ### Excuse Me?
>
> A presenter from a manufacturing company said, "We require that our manufacturing process results in a final product that fulfills our expectations with arrival at our customer's plant to coincide with their predetermined timetable."
>
> When I asked him exactly what that meant, he said, "We have to make a quality product and deliver it on time."

Only someone who truly knows his or her subject can say what he or she wants to say in clear and simple language.

> *"If you can't explain a complex subject simply, you don't understand it well enough. Nothing is so complex that it cannot be explained simply."*
>
> —Albert Einstein

Former Apple CEO Steve Jobs was considered one of our most electrifying communicators. In every presentation, instead of using the highly technical language he was so capable of speaking, he demonstrated his excitement by saying things such as:

- "We're going to show you some amazing stuff."

- "This is an awesome computer."

- "This is one of the coolest things we've done."

- "We're so excited to show you this. It's incredible."

If you want to be described as a clear and concise communicator, eliminate unnecessary words, simplify your phrases, and speak in short, declarative sentences. Avoid using acronyms. Speak conversationally, as you normally would. Strive for brevity and clarity. Audiences will appreciate what you said and that it took you so little time to say it.

Comfortable

The feelings a speaker exhibits affect how the audience feels. If the speaker is nervous or anxious, the audience will be uncomfortable. A speaker who exhibits the characteristic of comfort smiles easily and often. His or her manner is confident and determined but also friendly and relaxed. His or her vocal inflection is conversational, and the pace is unhurried.

Confident

Confidence is one of the most important characteristics exhibited by an excellent presenter. Confidence comes from a strong sense of self, from knowing you are prepared, and from believing that what you say will benefit those listening.

Confident speakers have excellent posture, square their shoulders, hold their heads up, and look directly at the audience so that each person feels they are speaking directly to them. Their movements are deliberate and purposeful. Their voices are strong and easily heard. They are focused and concise. They are comfortable with silence and pause strategically to let important points sink in. They handle questions thoroughly and handle even those who disagree with a quiet professionalism that says, "I am in control."

Confident speakers use short, declarative sentences and positive language. They avoid diminishing words and phrases that weaken their message—for example, "just," "a little bit," "maybe," or "I guess."

Convincing

To add "convincing" to the list of traits describing you as a presenter, think and present in a logical manner so that your audience won't have to guess where you are going.

To win over an audience and have them agree with your point of view, your message must make sense. Well presented points that lead logically to your goal will convince your audience, step by step, that you have done your homework, that you know what you are talking about, and that you believe in your solution.

Support your points with examples and experiences. Your message should be so well presented that your audience reaches your conclusion before you present it. Let them convince themselves.

> *"A problem well stated is a problem half solved."*
>
> —Charles F. Kettering,
> inventor, engineer, and businessman

Remember the visual and vocal elements. To be convincing you must appear and sound convinced. Use engaging eye contact and a strong voice to emphasize your main points.

Creative and Interesting

When an audience takes time to listen to what you have to say, you have no right to be boring. Memorable speakers present their ideas in a manner that engages and moves their audiences. They present ideas in a different, unexpected manner. They pepper their remarks with stories and anecdotal material. Often they use props to hold the interest of the audience.

Audiences respond best to pictures that are clearly planted in their minds. Speak in colorful "word pictures" that interestingly describe what you are talking about. Rather than saying "The building will be approximately twenty thousand square feet," say "The building will cover the entire city block." Instead of saying "This doughnut has thirty-two fat grams," say, "This doughnut has as much fat as three big scoops of Crisco." Better yet, show the audience three big scoops of Crisco.

In my presentation skills training sessions, I list the topics we have discussed over the two days and ask the participants to develop a short presentation about one of the topics. I am always amazed by the creativity shown in these short presentations. Two of them especially stand out in my mind.

Patrick McGowan's Presentation

Patrick McGowan, an analyst with Wells Fargo Advisors' Wealth, Brokerage, and Retirement division, walked to the front of the room and asked for a volunteer. One of his colleagues quickly joined him.

Patrick explained that he was going to ask his friend to solve simple and more difficult math problems out loud while his friend was also to keep track of how many times Patrick clicked the pen he held in his hand and switched the pen from hand to hand.

His colleague was impressive in how quickly he could solve the math problems as Patrick read them out loud one by one.

"What is one plus one?"

"What is five plus seven?"

"What is nine times four?"

"What is eleven squared?"

(story continues on next page)

(continued from previous page)

"What is the square root of two hundred fifty-six?"

When Patrick finished, his colleague had no idea how many times Patrick had clicked the pen or changed it from hand to hand even though Patrick was standing right in front of him.

Patrick's point? Multitasking kills our productivity. Human beings simply cannot do multiple things at the same time and do them all well.

Patrick White's Presentation

Patrick White was in the same class with Patrick McGowan. Patrick, a management metrics analyst with Wells Fargo Advisors, kept the audience intrigued as he silently walked to the front of room, looked at his watch, walked over to the easel and wrote on the pad, "Adam, what time does our plane land?"

He then motioned for his colleague, Adam, to come from his seat and write his answer on the board. Adam wrote "Ten a.m." on the board.

(story continues on next page)

(continued from previous page)

Patrick looked at his watch again and announced to the class, "That took forty-five seconds. Now let's try that another way."

He asked Adam, "What time does our plane land?"

Adam replied, "Ten a.m."

"Hmmm," said Patrick. "That took four seconds."

His point? E-mail can be a very inefficient way to communicate. Gee, you think? Now that's creativity!

Energetic

Nothing loses an audience faster than a presenter who stands in one place, speaking in a monotone, low-volume voice, with little or no expression on his or her face. That's when the BlackBerrys are pulled out and the audience turns to checking e-mail. I don't blame them. We simply will not suffer our time being wasted.

Energetic speakers move their bodies and hands expressively. They use their faces to exhibit their feelings. Their voices are easily heard. Their vocal inflection emphasizes what they are saying.

If you want to be an energetic presenter, be enthusiastic about your message and let your body naturally follow. Be careful, however, not to cross the line into theatrical. Too much energy can diminish your credibility and distract your audience. Controlled energy, on the other hand, can be quiet on the surface with a strong undercurrent.

What can you do to create energy when you're just not feeling it? Find a way to get your heart rate up and get oxygen flowing to your brain. A short run will do it, but if there's no opportunity for that, take a brisk walk up and down the hall.

My former partner and the founder of Wheless-Wyatt Communications, Bill Wheless, is a tall guy— around six foot three, I'm guessing. More than once I've seen him, on the way to a presentation he was delivering, jump up and down in the elevator. If there happened to be other people in the elevator, they flattened themselves against the walls as they wondered about this guy. But I knew what he was doing. He was pumping himself up, getting the energy flowing. Bill is fond of citing the Nike mantra "Just do it!"

Engaging

Effective speakers engage their audiences immediately in their opening remarks and keep them engaged throughout their presentations. The best way to do that is to consider why your message is of value to your audience. Tell them upfront; and throughout your presentation answer their question, "What's in this for me?"

Honest

An audience describes a speaker as honest when he or she comes across as believable and comfortable with what he or she does and does not know. The quickest way to lose credibility is to bluff your way through a question you can't answer. You'll be described as honest when you've exhibited your confidence by saying "I don't know." Once people have heard you say that, they will know that when you are answering a question, you believe your answer to be an honest and accurate one.

Knowledgeable

How can you come across as knowledgeable? You can actually *be* knowledgeable. This is a product of preparation. You should have researched your topic thoroughly and anticipated every question your audience may ask and have the accurate answers to those questions firmly in your mind. Your credibility will remain intact if someone asks you a question you can't answer if you simply say, "I don't know, but I'll find out and get back to you." Then make sure you follow up.

Once you've prepared, relax. You can't know everything. If you know what you should reasonably be expected to know, you'll be prepared.

Passionate

Speakers who are passionate about their subjects exude enthusiasm. You can see in their eyes and mannerisms and hear in their voices that they feel strongly. Passionate speakers engage their audiences and make them want to listen. If they feel this strongly about their subject, perhaps the audience should as well.

Sometimes salespeople who have a hard time feeling passionate about what they are selling will ask me if I have tips for selling a product they really don't believe is the best solution for the customer. Yes, I do. Find another job. In the long run, your customer will benefit, your company will benefit, and you'll benefit because you'll be able to sleep at night if you don't go against your own sense of honesty and ethics.

Personable

We have enough corporate robots out there. People relate to people. A speaker who comes across as a human being is both interesting and engaging. Too often presenters put on their "Mr. or Ms. Presenter" hat when they step in front of an audience, and their personalities disappear.

We are all unique. Our personalities are based on our own feelings, knowledge, thought processes, and life experiences. It may be our uniqueness that gets us hired in the first place. Yet too often, once we join a company, we soon talk, act, and think like everyone else. Allow the strength of who you are to influence your presentations and how you deliver them. I always tell my clients, "I want you to bring yourself with you when you present." Audiences relate to authenticity. Don't be afraid to be yourself in front of an audience. It's refreshing.

Relatable

Audiences must believe that the speaker knows them, can relate to their lives, and has a clear understanding of their circumstances. Speakers who seem to come from a totally different world hold no credibility and lose their audiences' attention, if they ever grabbed their attention in the first place.

To come across as relatable, you must know your audience. You must put yourself in their shoes by understanding their feelings and experiences. Your message should be from their point of view. Come across as someone who is empathetic and your audience will listen to what you have to say.

Prepared

There is simply no substitute for preparation. Audiences know a speaker is prepared when he or she exhibits confidence, delivers a logical and compelling message, and is ready for all reasonable questions. Nothing alleviates anxiety better than knowing you're adequately prepared.

Additional Considerations for Effective Delivery
Controlling Anxiety

> *"There are two types of speakers—those that are nervous and those that are liars."*
>
> —Mark Twain

You may have heard that public speaking is the number-one fear in America and that death is number six. I don't know if that's true, but it's believable enough. A great number of people fear speaking in front of others. This fear is found at all levels in business and in the private sector. Unfortunately, it is responsible for limiting careers. There is good news, however. Fear of public speaking can be overcome.

What Happens When We Become Anxious?

We are all created with a flight-or-fight response when we sense a threat. The moment we perceive a threat, an alarm goes off in our brain, which triggers secretions of two essential and effective stimulants, cortisol and adrenaline. As these stimulants course through our bodies, they increase our heart rate and body temperature and prepare the body to defend itself. Extra blood courses to our hands, legs, and brain, which primes our muscles and nervous system for action and causes our palms and forehead to sweat. Because the stomach is so vulnerable to attack, blood immediately leaves the area, which causes butterflies, nausea, and cramping. It is not pretty.

This stimulation, however, is exactly what we need to give us the energy and focus to deliver a fine presentation. We just need to control it.

Anxiety is nervous energy turned inward. Enthusiasm and vitality are the same energy turned outward. My former partner and company founder, Bill Wheless, often remarked, "We don't want to lose the butterflies. We just want them to fly in formation!"

When you feel anxiety coming on, welcome it. It's the energy you need to succeed. Professional presenters, just like entertainers and athletes, see the heebie-jeebies as a good thing—a sign that their minds and bodies are preparing themselves to be as enthusiastic and energetic as possible.

What Causes Anxiety?

- lack of preparation

- lack of a plan to control anxious feelings and symptoms

- lack of self-esteem

Preparation

There is absolutely nothing better to alleviate anxiety than having successful experiences behind you and knowing you are prepared. If you expect people to take their time and listen to you and you aren't prepared, you deserve every bit of anxiety you have. Preparation goes way back to the beginning when you consider your audience, establish a goal, and develop a logical and persuasive presentation that benefits those listening. It continues as you familiarize yourself with the room in which you will be presenting and rehearse your presentation. Preparation also includes thinking of everything that could possibly go wrong and having a plan to deal with it.

See the preparation checklist in Part 5 – Getting Started. You may want to revise it to meet your individual needs. While I believe you can be overly rehearsed, I do not believe there is any such thing as being overly prepared. In real estate the mantra is "Location, location, location." In presenting it's "Preparation, preparation, preparation."

Control

Knowing how to decrease how often you feel anxious and lessen anxious feelings will give you the confidence to move confidently forward.

- **Get your mind right with positive self-talk.** This is not the time to think negative thoughts. We create what we think about, so think about delivering a fine, focused presentation. Tell yourself that you are prepared and competent. Remind yourself that your audience will benefit from what you have to say.

- **Breathe deeply.** Take several slow, deep breaths, completely filling your lungs. This will increase the oxygen to your brain and calm you. Remember to breathe during your presentation!

- **Smile.** Facial expressions reflect how you feel, but they also can influence how you feel. When you feel good, you smile. When you smile, you feel good. So smile!

- **Have room-temperature water available.** Place it on the shelf inside the lectern or off to the side so your audience won't be distracted, wondering whether you might knock it over. When you need a drink, pause and take one confidently. Your audience will admire your "I'm in charge here" demeanor.

- **Dress comfortably and appropriately.** Pay particular attention to fit. You have enough on your mind without having to fidget with your clothes.

- **Watch what you eat and drink.** Avoid spicy foods that could cause gastric disturbances. Avoid caffeine, unless of course, you're a caffeine addict, in which case this isn't a good time to give it up! Drink plenty of water.

- **Get plenty of sleep.** If your anxiety is keeping you awake, this may be a good time for positive self-talk.

- **Slow down.** Anxiety often causes speakers to rush, often unknowingly but sometimes purposefully, just to get through it so they can sit down. Slow down and concentrate on what you are saying. Focus on the audience not your performance. Be more concerned with the audience "getting it" than how they may feel about your delivery. Remember, it's not about you. It's about the audience.

- **Use notes.** It's always better to have notes and not need them than to need them and not have them. There is nothing weak about having notes. They keep you on track, which audiences appreciate. If it makes you feel better to explain that, go ahead.

- **If you're nervous only at the beginning, consider opening your presentation by asking the audience a question.** This will take the focus off of you for a few minutes while you "defrost."

Attitude follows behavior. Act as if you're enjoying yourself and feeling confident, and you'll feel those feelings. When you believe in your message and use your own words to support it, your body (and mind) will respond naturally.

Self-Esteem

This topic sometimes keeps me up at night and often is heartbreaking. In my work as an executive coach and presentations skills trainer, I encounter many people who have a poor self-image and constantly tell themselves, *I can't. I'm not as good as so and so. I'll never be able to do this or that.*

Perhaps learning about the self-esteem challenges of my clients is common in my profession because effective leadership and speaking require a great deal of self-confidence. Senior leaders as well as entry-level professionals deal with this issue.

Eleanor Roosevelt once said, "No one can make you feel inferior without your permission." Yet so many of us walk around with a sign on our back that says, "Kick me." I want you to take that sign off.

I appreciate the messages of Pastor Joel Osteen, who has much to say on this topic. He tells a story of a group of three- and four-year-old children who were tested for creativity, innovation, and imagination. Ninety-five percent of the children rated extremely high. At age seven the children were tested again, but only 5 percent rated high in creativity, innovation, and imagination.

Why? What had happened to those children? Life happened. Somewhere along the way, someone had convinced them to question themselves and their abilities.

Another story Pastor Osteen tells is about how he accidentally slowed his computer down to a crawl so that it hardly worked at all. Innocently enough, like so many of us, he pushed a bunch of keys he wasn't familiar with which loaded his computer with all kinds of junk. He had to call the manufacturer and have his computer reset to the original manufacturer's settings. I believe this is what many of us should do from time to time—reset ourselves to our original manufacturer's settings.

Building Confidence

Confidence is your belief in your ability to succeed. Being prepared and having successful experiences behind you are two important keys to building confidence. How do you get successful experiences behind you? Here are some ideas:

- **Seize every opportunity to speak.** The more speaking you do, the more confident you become. The more confident you become, the more willing you are to speak. An opportunity to speak doesn't limit itself to a prepared business presentation. Any time an audience focuses on you, it is an opportunity, an experience that will boost your confidence. Look for such opportunities at team meetings, neighborhood association meetings, and book club gatherings. Be sure, however, that when you speak, you actually have something worthwhile to say.

- **Act as if you already are a confident presenter.** Attitude follows behavior. Dress, speak, and behave as a confident presenter. When you think and act as though something is true, you help make it so.

- **Realize you have something to say.** When you've considered your audience and the value of your message to them, realize that what you have to say is of benefit. Trust that you have done your homework and are knowledgeable about the topic. This should increase your self-assurance. Trust yourself as the presenter, and you will project confidence. (If you don't have something of value to say, you shouldn't be speaking.)

- **Get your anxiety under control.** (See the section on anxiety earlier in this book.)

- **Meet your audience in advance.** Whenever possible, a good way to lessen your anxiety is to arrive early and meet your audience as they enter the room. Introduce yourself, shake hands, smile, and look them in the eye. You'll be surprised at how this rids you of nervousness. It also sets the tone for a relaxed, natural delivery. It will make your presentation seem more like an extended conversation among friends.

- **Understand that your audience is on your side.** It helps to remember that you and your audience are on the same team. Rather than critiquing your speaking abilities, they're concentrating on your message and how it can benefit them. If you deliver a fine, focused presentation, the audience wins, too.

- **Rehearse, rehearse, and rehearse.** The word "rehearse" means to re-hear. As you rehearse, your brain familiarizes itself with your message. You become comfortable with the words and phrases you will use. You gain confidence in the equipment you are using and your ability to handle the mechanics seamlessly, which allows you to focus instead on your audience.

You will want to rehearse to make sure your presentation isn't too long. Have your rehearsed message finish at about 20 percent less time than you have been given. An audience will always appreciate your finishing early, but they probably will not tolerate your going over. If someone presenting before you got the meeting off track by going too long, be the professional and finish early, which will get everything back on schedule. If you've rehearsed a shorter version, you'll know how to do that, to eliminate part of your presentation without shortchanging your audience. It is very "real life" to show up at a presentation and have the client say, "Gee, Linda, we thought we had thirty minutes, but we're running a little long. Can you do your presentation in fifteen minutes instead?"

I've heard people say, "I don't have time to rehearse." You don't have to rehearse all your presentations, just the important ones. If every interaction leaves people with an impression, aren't they all important?

I once stood with a company president and his team at an industry conference. The company president remarked that he never rehearsed his presentations; he would just "wing" them. He said, They always turn out fine." I wish you could have heard his team when he walked away. "He thinks they turn out fine," they said, "but the truth is that when he stands up to talk, we all tune out and take that time to think about something else."

Here's the bottom line. You're going to rehearse your presentations. The question is whether your audience will be sitting there when you do it. That isn't the time to find out what doesn't work. If you want to stand out as a presenter, have enough respect for your audiences to be the best you can be when you call them to be on the other side of you.

- **Visualize your success.** Before any presentation, mentally walk your body and emotions through your talk. See yourself speaking with confidence and poise. Hear yourself speaking with eloquence. Feel your energy as you stand before an enthusiastic audience. Your body will respond to the pictures you hold in your mind.

The mind cannot distinguish between what is real and what is vividly imagined. Remember, you create what you think about. If you have visualized a successful presentation, when it is time for the real thing, your confidence will be strong because it will seem as though you've been there before and that you have a successful experience behind you.

Can You Imagine?

One of my favorite stories about visualization tells of a basketball team that was practicing free throws.

Half the team went to one end of the gym to practice; the other half went to the opposite end. One group had a ball; the other group didn't.

The group without the ball vividly imagined each step of their practice. They imagined themselves standing in just the right spot. They "felt" the ball in their hands and "saw" it leave their hands with just the right arch to land in the exact middle of the net. They "heard" the swoosh as the ball fell through the net and the thud as it bounced on the floor.

When the two groups got back together, the group that had practiced without a ball had improved every bit as much as the group that had practiced with a ball.

In Front of Your Audience

Much of what has been covered so far takes place prior to the delivery of your presentation, including:

- discovering how you come across

- learning details about your audience and meeting site

- establishing your goal

- preparing your message

- considering the use of visual aids and how to design them

- understanding the impact of your visual and vocal delivery

- exhibiting the characteristics of a winning presenter

- controlling anxiety and building confidence

Now that you're ready to step in front of the audience, what else is there to know that will affect your success?

Appearance

As unfair as it seems, others judge us by our appearance. Appearance contributes significantly to how we come across to other people who are deciding whether we are believable as communicators.

Many things contribute to our appearance – how we stand, how we move, how we make eye contact, facial expression, etc. For now, let's talk about dress.

When you're in front of an audience, the rule is the same for men and women.

> **If they remember what you are wearing, you are wearing the wrong thing.**

You want people to listen to what you are saying, not critique what you are wearing. Since you are always presenting, always sending a signal, this applies anytime you are in the workplace. While you may want to dress according to your unique personality, you should be able to express your uniqueness and still adopt a professional style. The workplace is for serious, not sexy. Consider how you want to come across. If being promoted is in your plan, give serious consideration to how you are dressed and groomed. For our purposes, let's discuss a few basics that apply to both men and women.

- Your clothes should be clean, pressed, and fit you well. Buy the best quality you can afford, and include classic styles rather than trendy fashions. If necessary have your clothes altered. It is well worth the investment. Even an expensive suit will look sloppy if the sleeves are too long.

- Wear garments that are understated and match your demeanor with a quiet professionalism, rather than scream, "Look at me!"

- Pay particular attention to your shoes. I've seen some nicely dressed professionals whose entire look was destroyed by unpolished, scuffed, worn-out shoes. The condition of your shoes says a lot about you.

- When presenting, remove anything that is hanging from you—for example a cell phone, name tag, security badge, a pen in your pocket, or anything that might attract the attention of the audience.

- Dress to mirror your audience but just a notch above. If you show up to speak to a group of plant workers who are all dressed in denim, and you're dressed in the most executive appearance you can achieve, they will not relate to you. Tone it down. While dressing to the audience is important, never forget that you are representing your organization.

Setting the Tone

As the presenter you can set the tone of the meeting—whether it's serious, high-energy, or casual. You set the tone with your dress, demeanor, the sound of your voice, your eye contact, and how you use your body.

You'll want to make sure your tone matches your message or your words will not ring true. Men can quickly change their tone from serious to casual simply by removing their jackets and ties and rolling up their shirtsleeves. A hand in the pocket also sends a relaxed message. Women have to plan ahead.

I Don't Believe You

I'll never forget what Bill Wheless, founder of Wheless-Wyatt Communications, did with an executive client in 1996.

We were working with a state bank president and his direct reports in a two-day presentation skills workshop. The president (I'll call him Walter) got up to deliver a prepared presentation to the group for critiquing. As the audience, we were to pretend we were a group of new employees.

Walter was tall and athletic. He was dressed in a very executive style, with a dark suit; a white, straight-collar shirt; a small-patterned tie; and highly shined, lace-up shoes. His hair was neither too long nor too short. (There's about one day within every six weeks when that happens, yet every time I saw Walter his hair looked perfect.) There was not a speck of lint on him anywhere, and I believe it was that way at all times.

(story continues on next page)

(continued from previous page)

Walter stood with perfect posture behind the lectern and told funny story after story about how he had messed up on his way up the corporate ladder. The problem was that his words didn't ring true. He looked every bit the perfect bank president who couldn't mess up if he tried.

Bill Wheless, in his wisdom, asked Walter to remove his jacket, pull out a table, and lean against it as he repeated his presentation.

As Walter began again, his voice softened; he got a twinkle in his eye; the whole room relaxed with him. He looked like he actually could relate to the audience of new employees. He had been in our shoes. Walter reached his goal—to have the audience know they will make mistakes along the way and it will all be fine.

We are always sending signals.

Movement

Nothing is more boring than a presenter who hides behind the lectern. (Of course, if the microphone is affixed and you were not able to secure a lavaliere microphone, you have no choice. But let's just suppose that isn't the case.)

Many presenters feel more comfortable hanging onto the lectern and having that barrier between them and their audience. Their attention, in this case, is on themselves and not on their audience.

Movement creates interest. Move from behind the lectern and walk toward your audience, making a connection. When you need to see your notes, move back toward the lectern, glance down to get what you need, and come back out again.

When you move, do so with purpose. Move toward someone to make a connection, and then return to the front of the room without turning your back to your audience.

Be careful not to rock or pace. Repetitive movement can be very distracting. Movement should be for a reason.

When you're making a point or saying something you want to reinforce, stand still. You don't want to be walking on your best stuff. When standing still, stand with your weight evenly on both feet. Stand up straight with your head held up and your shoulders back.

Eye Contact

Eye contact is the conduit through which communication takes place. If you ever read a book that instructs you to "just look over their heads" if you're uncomfortable making eye contact, I hope you will ignore that detrimental piece of advice. In this country eye contact is critical to effective communication. It is how we as human beings connect. There's an old saying that "the eyes are the window to the soul." It certainly is difficult to "read" someone if they don't look you in the eye.

Making eye contact will help you read the effect your message has on your audience and help you respond appropriately. It also will help you come across as authoritative and confident. Making appropriate eye contact keeps your audience engaged and shows that you have a genuine interest in each person. Make contact with as many people in the audience as you can and as often as you can. If the crowd is large, look to the back corners as though you can see the people sitting there. Be careful, however, not to look like a sprinkler going back and forth and side to side. Contact means just that—connection.

How long should you hold eye contact? There is no rule. You'll know when it is right. Eye contact should be two people seeing each other seeing each other. When you have done that, you can move on.

Be aware of differences in culture concerning eye contact. In some countries, for example, making eye contact is considered disrespectful.

Facial Expression

So much can be read in a person's face. It shows every emotion. As a communicator, be aware of the message your face sends, and be sure you send the message you intend to send. If you tell your audience you are convinced, but the look on your face says otherwise, they will not believe you.

Remember that facial expression and eye contact contribute to the visual clues that determine 55 percent of your believability.

The popular use of Botox to paralyze the facial muscles in an effort to keep wrinkles from forming has caused quite a problem. With no facial expression to read, one can misinterpret a speaker's intention, which can lead to misunderstandings. Advances in communication technology, such as PowerPoint, which takes the focus off the presenter's face, and e-mail and conference calls, in which facial expression is absent, are destroying communication in many cases. And now with Botox, advances in science and medicine may be doing the same thing.

Using Your Hands

I don't often see presenters use their hands too much, although many people feel that they do. Hand movement is a natural expression of our emotions, and frequently our gestures aid our meaning without our thinking too much about it.

You can help an audience stay with you by gesturing the number of the point you are making. You can paint a picture with your hand gestures. For example you might say, "He was really tall" while holding your hand above your head or say, "The whole country" with your hands spread apart in a wide gesture. This kind of movement makes you interesting.

If you're conscious of your hands and really don't know what to do with them, try the following. Hold a pen or a remote control or a pair of glasses comfortably with both hands together a little above waist high. (This height will keep your shoulders from rounding forward.) Your hands will have something to do. You can gesture easily with either hand, and they'll have a place to return. Be sure you don't pop the pen or tap it or play with it. If you're prone to fidgeting, find something to hold that won't tempt you.

Pausing

The mark of a professional is someone who is comfortable with silence. Too often speakers fill the "air" between sentences or during transitions with non-words such as "um" or "uh." Often they don't know they are doing it, and it can be a real favor to point it out to them. If they do this in everyday conversation, you can bet they'll do it in front of an audience. An occasional "um" doesn't hurt, but it can be distracting when said often.

For some, awareness that this is an issue is all a speaker needs to solve it. For others it can be a difficult habit to break. If you're challenged by the use of non-words, enlist the help of family, friends, and colleagues to help you break the habit by asking them to tell you when they hear you say these non-words. Diligent attention could solve this problem, and your audiences will appreciate it.

Well-placed pauses allow your audience to stay with you. Certainly you should pause between your sentences.

Pause, Please!

In one of my training classes, a presenter was having trouble slowing down. All his sentences ran together. When I asked him to pause between sentences, he was still having trouble.

"Just say one-one-thousand, two-one-thousand before you start your next sentence," I suggested.

That is exactly what he did. He began his presentation again, and at the end of the first sentence, he recited out loud, "One-one-thousand, two-one thousand." (I don't make this stuff up.)

Pause when you transition from one part of your presentation to another. It lets your audience know you are finished with that section and are moving on.

Pauses can make an impact if you pause as you state something you feel is important. Let your words sit for a bit before moving on. The pause will add strength to what you just said.

When you pause when presenting, just as you do in everyday conversation, you exhibit a natural pace and tone. You come across as connected to your message and your audience rather than sound like someone who is just reciting words.

Answering Questions

My guess is that 99 percent of presenters who entertain questions from the audience take the questions after their closing remarks. Let me tell you why this isn't a good idea. We remember best what we hear first, second best what we hear last, and least best what we hear in the middle. In the middle is where you've put your most important points, then you summarize them in your close so your audience will walk away remembering what you want them to remember (what you said last). If you deliver your summarizing close and then take questions, someone may ask a question that derails what you said, or they may bring up something that will take the focus off your message. If that happens, that is what the audience may walk out remembering.

It's wiser to ask for questions, and then close, summarizing your main points and telling the audience what to do as a result of having heard your message.

When someone asks a question, begin your answer to that person, and then, as you are answering, make eye contact with others in the room. This way your audience will remain engaged. A one-on-one conversation between you and the questioner gives others in the room an opportunity to take a mental exit, and you might not be able to get their attention back.

Unfortunately you may from time to time encounter a hostile questioner or someone who wants to be argumentative. No matter how dumb or trivial their question is or how disruptive they want to be, don't let them engage you. Chances are that others in the audience have seen this kind of behavior from this person before, and it may be that he or she doesn't really want an answer; they just want to see if they can rattle you.

You will come out ahead every time if you remain calm and professional and resist the temptation to shoot back. For example you might say, "Susan, I see this is important to you, and I appreciate your thoughts. I think we should explore this in more detail, but to keep this meeting on time, let's move on now to my second point." Then immediately make eye contact with someone else and continue your presentation.

> *"Nothing gives one person so much advantage over another as to remain always cool and unruffled under all circumstances."*
>
> —Thomas Jefferson

If someone asks you a question you can't answer, don't bluff your way through it. Remember what was said earlier in this book about honesty and credibility? You will only lose your credibility one time. You can throw the question to the audience, but don't single someone out to answer it, because you may put him or her on the spot. For example you might say, "I don't know, Brad. Can anyone answer Brad's question?" If no one can answer the question, tell Brad you'll find out and get back to him. Then add to your credibility by following through with your commitment.

If you ask for questions following your presentation and there aren't any, it might be because your message was perfectly clear or because no one understood or cared about a word you said. Either way it's an awkward moment. To avoid this, have a question of your own to get you back into your close. For example you might say, "You may wonder what would happen if..." or "Sometimes people are concerned about such an aggressive timeline. Let me address that."

Answer all questions thoroughly, but don't speak beyond the question. You could open up an entirely new discussion you hadn't planned (or wanted) to get into.

Working With Notes

If you've printed your notes on four-by-six-inch cards, hold them just above waist high. When you need to reference them, look at them without dropping your head.

If you've printed your notes on eight-and-a-half-by-eleven sheets, carry them in a leather portfolio. Place them on a lectern or table rather than holding them in your hand. If you're away from the lectern when it's time to reference your notes, move back to where you can see them before you need to be there. You don't want your audience sitting in silence while you walk back to your notes. Glance down, see what you need to see, and then return your focus to your audience.

Instead of flipping pages over, slide them from right to left. You will then have two pages of notes visible. Turn up the left lower corners of your pages so you can easily grab a page as you slide it over.

Notes will help you stay on track. It is important to have them; however, they should not be handled in a manner that will distract the audience.

Delivery Using Visual Aids

Delivering Your Message Using PowerPoint

So you have developed your presentation; determined that PowerPoint slides will add interest, clarify, or otherwise aid the audience; and effectively designed your slides. You're only halfway there.

During your presentation, you must present your slides in a seamless, professional manner so you won't have "the props taking over from the actor, the apparatus from the magician" ("An Electrifying Presentation," John O'Toole, *Selling* magazine, October 1993).

Nothing loses an audience faster than letting them sit there while the presenter familiarizes himself with the equipment or works out an issue when it doesn't work as expected.

Whenever possible, rehearse your presentation in the room you will be using, with the equipment you will be using. On the day of your presentation, arrive long before your audience to prepare your equipment and make sure everything works smoothly. If the room is being used prior to your meeting, you'll have to get creative. Do whatever it takes to ensure that you never step in front of an audience without being familiar with how to work the equipment.

Some large meeting venues have audio-visual technicians who can advance your slides for you. It is imperative that you communicate clearly so you won't have a slide coming up before you're ready for it. You will come across as much more polished if you can avoid saying, "Next slide, please." This will require a clear understanding between you and the technician about how you will transition from one point to the next and exactly when you want the slides to appear and to go away. When speaking, I prefer to advance the slides myself. As the presenter, that should be your choice.

If the room will allow it, arrange it so that you will be standing to your audience's left. Because we read left to right, it will be easier for them to look at you and then look at the screen, moving from left to right.

Be careful not to block the screen, either with your body, the lectern, or anything else. Before the audience arrives, sit in the seats that may be blocked from the screen to determine if there will be an issue, and, if so, take care of it. If your audience has a bad experience, it will reflect on you as a presenter.

Blocking the Screen

Once when I was critiquing a presenter, I told him he was blocking the screen. His reply was, "But I think that adds mystery!"

Motion attracts people's eyes. Gesture to the screen when you want the audience to look there. Stand still when you want them to focus on the screen. Move when you want to capture their attention again.

Avoid reading your slides to the audience. Your slides should complement what you say (add to or make stronger); they should not *be* what you say. Too often presenters turn their backs on the audience and read the slides word for word. This is how we put children to sleep; we read to them.

If you want your audience to read what is on the slide, be quiet and give them a chance to do that. Don't talk until they've had a chance to digest the slide. Tell the audience what they will see before you put the slide up and what you want them to get from the slide. For example you might say, "Next you'll see the timeline for this project. Note the compressed time between steps three and four." Then put the slide up and give your audience time to familiarize themselves with it before you talk.

Here's another example: "This is what I think we all should consider." Then put up a slide with a quote or statement on it, and remain quiet while the audience reads it.

Keep your eyes forward, connecting with the audience. It can become a bad habit to keep looking at the screen. When you do that, you lose contact with your audience, and they can lose your voice as your face is turning away from them. You should know what is coming up next (remember to rehearse). Position your laptop from which you are projecting your visuals so you can see the laptop screen but your audience can't. To make sure the correct visual is projecting, glance at your laptop instead of turning around to look at the screen.

You should not have a slide up the entire time you are talking. Remember that *you* are the presentation, not your visuals. To present seamlessly using PowerPoint, place a black slide between the ones you want to show. (There may be a more technical way to create a black slide, but I simply fill in the background of a blank slide with black.) When you've finished with a slide and want the audience's attention back on you, advance to the black slide. You will see all eyes turn your way.

When projecting, if you want the audience's attention temporarily back on you and you'll be returning to the same slide, hit the "B" key on your computer keyboard or the blank-the-slide button on your remote. When you hit the key again, the current slide will still be on the screen.

It's important to have a plan for delivering your presentation without visual support. Always have a printout of your slides to use as your notes if necessary. Rehearse delivering your presentation without visuals. That could become necessary should an equipment failure occur. Resist telling the audience that you had visuals, but they don't work. They will feel shortchanged, and your presentation is probably better without them anyway. You should have prepared and rehearsed your "uh-oh" presentation so well that your audience will believe this is what you intended all along.

If you're sending your slides in advance to be projected from someone else's computer, have them on a flash drive with you just in case something goes wrong. Expect things to go wrong and be prepared.

Delivering Your Message Using Handouts

Just as with PowerPoint slides, remember that anything you put between you and your audience can be a distraction. We simply cannot do two things at once (e.g., listen to the presenter and read a handout). If you feel a handout, passed out before or as you are talking, is a good idea, know what you will be giving up.

It is highly unlikely that your audience will stay with you as you advance through a handout, even if you ask them nicely to stay with you. As soon as the handout is in front of them, they will flip through it. In the case of a sales presentation, your client will go directly to the back page to see the cost before you have an opportunity to justify it.

Instead of giving out your handout before you begin and having your audience's eyes down in it as you start your presentation, you can:

- tell your audience you have all your supporting data in a handout for them to take with them as they are leaving

- pass out only the pages you really need them to see during the presentation

- pass out the handout and ask them to leave it facedown for now and then say, "Please turn to page one and note the diagram." Some will politely do as they are asked; some will move ahead.

- e-mail the handout in advance and ask them to familiarize themselves with it prior to the meeting and have their comments and questions ready. If you do this, know that they probably won't follow through with your request unless you are very specific with your expectations. More likely they will bring the handout with them and read it once you start talking, and sending it in advance will have accomplished nothing.

Delivering Your Message Using an Easel and Pad

When using an easel and pad, remember that you are the presenter. Position yourself in the center of the stage or room with the easel beside you—to your left if you are right-handed; to your right if you are left handed.

You may have prepared your presentation in advance on the pad. If so, make sure a couple of clean sheets are in front of your presentation so it won't show through before you're ready for the audience to see it. If you planned to draw as your presentation progresses, you can pencil in lightly on the paper in advance so you'll have an outline to follow that the audience can't see. Design it on notepaper first to save paper; pads for easels are expensive.

A tip my clients love is to have your talking points on a sticky note on the back of the easel. You can glance at your notes without your audience ever seeing you do it. Make sure the sticky note is affixed securely. It would be embarrassing to have it fall off and blow around on the floor as you are speaking.

If you have several sheets to refer to, in order to avoid a lot of flipping back and forth, you can look like a real pro. Place a paper clip on the sheet in front of what you want to show. Then, when you are ready to go there, slip your thumb behind the paper clip and flip all the unneeded pages over at once. Seamless! Your audience will never know how you did it. Don't put the paper clip on the page you want to show or your audience will see it and wonder what you have attached to the back of the page. (We can be distracted by anything.)

Here is the rule for writing on an easel and pad while you are presenting.

Touch, turn, talk.

If you tell your audience what you are going to write on the pad and then turn around and write it, while you are doing that, your audience is learning nothing new. But if you say, "Today we are going to talk about..." and then write on the pad, "2013 budget," they will stay right with you as you are writing. When you've finished writing, turn around, make eye contact and talk to your audience.

When you're finished with the easel and pad, turn over the used sheets and set the easel aside. If you leave the sheet you wrote on showing, your audience will continue to look at it.

Practice!

The keys to presenting effectively while using visuals are preparation, rehearsal, and practice. You will want to be so familiar with the equipment that you don't have to give operating it a second thought. Strive for a seamless presentation.

"We will never do a thing well until we cease to think about the manner of doing it."

—William Hazlitt,
nineteenth-century essayist

You're On!

It's time to begin.

If you will be introduced, stand as close as you can to where you will be speaking (and still be out of the way) so the audience won't have to wait for you to come from the back of the room. If you will introduce yourself, move with energy to the spot from which you will begin, smiling as you do so. Be genuine. If your presentation is going to be bad news, a broad smile will not be appropriate.

Carry your notes in a leather portfolio and have them placed where you want them before you start speaking so your face is not down as you arrange your notes. Make eye contact with your audience, project your voice to the back wall, engage everyone with your well-rehearsed open, and you are on your way.

Part 4 - Related Topics

~~~~~~

You are always presenting. As a communicator, you'll find yourself in a variety of situations that will require you to quickly discipline your thoughts, establish a goal, and selectively consider what to say to achieve that goal. In all of the related topics that follow, you'll find a recurring theme: It's about the audience.

First Impressions:
Opportunities to Shine or Fail

◇◇

No matter how good you get at the mechanics of presenting, true communication is a two-way street. What you say will be filtered through your listener's impression of you. Whoever said, "You only get one chance to make a good first impression" certainly had it right. You see, we don't want to be wrong.

If I met you yesterday and you were warm, attentive, friendly, and welcoming, I would form an impression about you based on that experience. If I saw you today and you were cold, aloof, and self-absorbed, I'd be more prone to believe you were just having a bad day, based on my first impression. If, however, I met you yesterday and you were cold, aloof, and self-absorbed, that impression would stick with me. If today you were friendly and welcoming, I would tend to believe you were being a fake.

We don't like for our beliefs to be challenged, to feel we are wrong. This is why it is so difficult to change a first impression. It may take many subsequent encounters to erase those initial thoughts. Many things contribute to a good first impression, but the most important is the following:

Care more about how you make others feel than about how you feel. When you have a genuine interest in the people around you, when you look them in the eye, listen intently, and inquire about subjects that are important to them, they will leave feeling good about themselves and their encounter with you.

From the discussion of Dr. Mehrabian's three V's of communication in Part 3 of this book, we know that appearance contributes to your believability. It also can affect a first impression. Your appearance should reflect that you respect yourself, that you take care of yourself, and that you make an effort to be pleasing to others. I'm not talking about movie-star good looks. While attractiveness contributes to likability, it contributes less than emotional expression and the ability to interact with others. While being beautiful certainly is nice, charisma takes the prize.

When you feel good about yourself, your confidence, poise, and energy will be infectious and draw people to you. Smiling makes you accessible and approachable. Facial expression can alter the temperature of blood that flows to the brain and change the way you feel. When you feel good, you smile. When you smile, you feel good. Let people see a welcoming look on your face.

If you genuinely want people to walk away with a good impression of you, remember the following:

> It's not about you. It's about how you make other people feel. They may forget what you said and what you did, but they will never forget how you made them feel.

Impromptu Speaking

> *"It usually takes me more than three weeks to write a good impromptu speech."*
>
> —Mark Twain

Speaking impromptu, without preparation or advance thought, accounts for about 99 percent of what we say. Therefore, it's important to learn to be organized in our thoughts so we can quickly and accurately deliver them.

Impromptu speaking is often referred to as speaking "off the cuff." This term is believed to have originated with waiters, who were among the first people to use their shirt cuffs as notepads to take orders or calculate a tab. Shirt cuffs were also handy for speakers to jot down notes during a meal and deliver their remarks afterward from arm's length.

Speaking without preparation or advance thought means being spontaneous. As contradictory as it sounds, spontaneity takes a great deal of preparation and rehearsal.

We live in a headline society. Being able to bottom-line your thinking will help make you a top-line success. Consider the thirty-second television commercial. In that time a company must:

- catch us

- keep us

- convince us

If you can't focus when you're speaking, you can bore us for minutes when you could have interested us in seconds. It bears repeating that if you can't say it in thirty seconds, you probably can't say it at all.

Speaking impromptu requires a lot of practice. (I know that doesn't seem to make sense, but stick with me here.) The more you practice, the more you will be able to speak clearly, logically, and with purpose.

You may be asking, "How do I practice something when I don't know what I'm going to be asked to speak about?" Great question. An impromptu speech (or answering a question or giving your opinion) is simply a mini-speech; therefore it has an open, middle, and close.

Here's what to practice:

1. **Listen.** Make sure you are clear about what the questioner is asking you—in other words, what they

want from you. Ask for clarification if you're unsure. Asking the questioner to repeat the question can buy you some time, or you can repeat the question yourself.

Take time to collect your thoughts. Relax. Take deep breaths. Silence your inner critical voice. Walk slowly to the lectern or stand behind your chair— whatever will give you a bit of time. Don't feel rushed. Most of us begin to speak before we have a clue what we will say. If silence makes you uncomfortable, you could say, "Let me consider that a moment before I answer." Then continue to move toward the front of the room or stand so the questioner won't move on without hearing from you.

2. **Don't begin to speak until you have a *goal* for what you want to say.** What do you want to achieve?

3. **Think of an engaging first sentence.** If you have time, write this sentence down and keep it solidly in your head. It is the most important thing you will say because it will either have your audience listening or tuning you out.

4. **Think of a few statements that will support your position and help you achieve your goal.** Jot down a few bullet points so you won't forget what you wanted to say. A good way to keep yourself on track is to think of an acronym whose letters will remind you of your points. Make sure your points are in a logical order.

5. **Close by coming back to your goal.**

Let me give you a couple of examples. In one of my presentation skills workshops, we were practicing speaking impromptu using the above steps. We'd write a word on the board and quickly call on someone to speak on the subject. The first woman called upon did an outstanding job of coming up with a goal, developing an engaging first sentence, following with reasons to support her goal, and coming back to her goal.

The word on the board was "fish." She slowly rose from her chair, taking time to walk to the front of the room. She paused before speaking and then looked at the audience and said, "I bet most of you have something in your freezer that is more valuable than cash" (engaging first sentence). She continued, "Most of you have fish in your freezer. If you eat fish three times a week, it will lower your blood pressure, help prevent cancer, and..." (She listed other benefits and reached her goal.) "So I hope you will consider eating more fish," she said in closing, "because fish can keep you healthy, and that's more valuable than cash because cash can't buy good health." (She closed by referring to her opening.)

Her goal was to get people to eat more fish. She thought of that first, then came up with an engaging first sentence. Then she added her points to get her to her goal and closed by stating her goal.

The next participant was a man. He took the same approach with the word "fish," but had a different message. He said, "You can have a fabulous vacation with your family and spend practically no money doing it" (engaging first sentence). He continued, "Have you ever thought of taking your kids fishing? Nothing excites a child more than sitting on a bank or dock with Mom or Dad and seeing that little fish jumping around on the end of his line as he pulls it out of the water. Those are memories you and your child will never forget." (This got him to his goal.) He closed by saying, "So I hope you'll think of fishing the next time you want an unforgettable time with your family." His goal was to let people know about an inexpensive activity, fishing, that would be enjoyable and memorable.

Think in terms of brevity and clarity.

Feel and act confident. Smile at the audience. Deliver your thoughts slowly to give yourself time to think and the audience time to absorb your information. Talk directly to the audience and adapt to their feedback. Maintain eye contact. Be brief; don't ramble or say too much on the subject. Speak at the audience's level. Don't try to memorize what you will say (with the exception of the first sentence). Memorizing will add to your anxiety because you'll be concentrating on the words and not on the message. Keep it conversational.

Can you apply this to business? Of course you can. Think of opportunities that come up in the course of your day. List as many potential questions as you can, and work with those. Practice thinking quickly of a goal, an engaging first sentence, supporting statements, and a closing. Before long it will become second nature to you.

Some people find it helpful to use the **PREP** System.

- **P: point** ("The point I want to make is...")
- **R: reason** ("The reason I say this is...")
- **E: example/experience** ("For example my experience is...")
- **P: point** ("In summary, my point is...")

Here's another exercise if, practiced daily, will bring focus to your day, and you'll know it so clearly that you'll be able to speak in an organized manner. Ask yourself:

1. What are the top issues on my plate today?
2. Why are they top priority?
3. What's the current status of these issues?
4. What outcome do I want?

One of my workshop participants, Carl, having been through our class only the day before and learning the above, called us enthusiastically to tell us the CEO of his company, whom he rarely sees, was in the elevator that morning when Carl stepped in. The CEO asked Carl how things were going in his division. Having started his day with the above exercise, Carl clearly and concisely answered the CEO's question, leaving the CEO feeling that Carl was really on top of things and definitely the right person for the job.

Unfortunately, when asked how things are going, most of us usually just say, "Fine" and kick ourselves later for having missed an opportunity.

When you develop the skill of impromptu thinking, it will become second nature to you. It will create a whole new mind-set. You may never again stumble through an opportunity to show how together you really are.

Presenting Effectively and Seamlessly as a Group

Though presenting as a group can require a lot of prep work, the ability to lead a group through a cohesive and energetic presentation is a skill appreciated by audiences and team members alike.

A good group leader is key. He or she should make sure there is a common goal for the presentation and that all team members contribute to that goal in a cohesive style. If each team member is simply assigned a part of the presentation to present as they wish, it will result in a choppy, disorganized mess, with the lack of effort apparent to the audience.

Know in advance how many people will be in the audience and don't have more presenters than audience members. If you do, your audience will feel overwhelmed.

Each person in the group should have something to contribute. Select people who can present effectively with conciseness, clarity, interest, and logic. When deciding who should present which topics, consider their skills and your objectives. If it will be a sales presentation, the person who will handle the business should lead the presentation and demonstrate their leadership ability. Give starring roles to those who present well and use others to answer key questions. This is a time for teamwork, not jockeying for individual visibility. The goal should be an effective outcome. Be sure techies or number crunchers don't talk over the heads of the people in the audience. Their mission is to provide answers or clarify, not to demonstrate how smart they are.

Prior to the presentation, the group leader or meeting organizer should introduce the group and each member. He or she should tell the audience enough about each person to relay what expertise is represented should they have a question.

Once group members are selected and topics assigned, structure the presentation to flow fluidly from one speaker to the next. Transition from one presenter to the next smoothly, without saying something like "And now Bill is going to take over." Rather, the finishing speaker should sum up his or her points and close, letting the next speaker begin by explaining how the previous presenter's information relates to what's coming up.

As part of the preparation, the entire group should consider any and all probable questions, agree on the answers, and agree on who will answer which questions and on how to direct an unexpected question.

Rehearsing as a group is critical. Having a volunteer audience to critique and give you feedback is invaluable. Rehearse for a seamless delivery and to ensure that the presentation ends on time. Rehearsing will ensure that the group operates as a smoothly functioning team.

Attention to details such as thoughtful selection of team members, preparation, and rehearsal will set your group presentation apart from those that are so predictably disjointed and, all too often, totally ineffective.

Traits of an Effective Facilitator/Trainer
On Time, On Task

An effective facilitator or trainer

1. introduces the topic clearly
2. creates a sense of importance about the topic and answers the audience's question, "Why do I need to know this and how will it help me?"
3. has a simple, achievable goal for the session ("If I am successful, what will have happened?")
4. uses good language skills:
    - a strong voice that can be easily heard and demonstrates authority

    - clarity

    - colorful language that uses anecdotal material, stories, metaphors, and examples

    - little or no jargon or acronyms

    - generous, well-placed pauses designed to increase understanding, which allows participants time to think

5. uses visuals effectively as an aid to understanding

6. exhibits high energy and confidence in his or her ability to do the job
7. demonstrates effective body language:
   - open gestures

   - movement with energy and purpose

   - eye contact

   - effective facial expression

8. has a good sense of time and moves things along
9. is sensitive to audience response and involvement:
   - doesn't allow one person to dominate

   - involves those who are reluctant to participate

   - engages the audience and makes them think

   - asks effective, thought-provoking questions

   - demonstrates patience

   - listens attentively to questions and concerns

10. has the ability to stay in control
11. is effective in pulling everything together, closing the discussion, drawing conclusions, summarizing key points, and creating an action plan

Handling Objections

Regardless of what we do for a living, we are all salespeople. We go through our day constantly selling our ideas to others and wanting them to see things our way and commit. From that perspective, let's consider our ability to handle objections just as one would if he or she were selling for a living. Apply these same ideas when you are communicating your ideas to others and encouraging them to see your point of view.

Change How You Feel About Objections

The best way to learn to handle objections is to first decide how you feel about them. They can cause you stress and anxiety and actually stall you and keep you from wanting to get in front of your clients/colleagues, or you can see objections in a positive light.

Any salesperson who would actually enjoy a position in which he or she doesn't have to deal with difficult questions and challenges would do well at a ballpark selling hotdogs and peanuts. In general people are rewarded for the amount of difficulty that goes with what they do. Wouldn't you rather be on top, facing numerous objections throughout your day, than at the bottom with no adversity but making no money?

If a prospect or listener says "no" but doesn't give you any reasons, your sale or conversation is over. If, however, they offer objections, you have an opportunity to redirect your presentation.

Hearing objections is a natural part of selling. There is nothing to brag about if you make a sales presentation and there isn't a single objection. Chances are that you didn't make the sale either. It's definitely not a good sign when a prospect sits silently, nodding his or her head as you drone on and on. If the client is considering buying, naturally he or she will have questions, and any objections will be a way of telling you what may need to change to make the sale a good fit.

Objections give you the opportunity to hone your sales skills. The more objections you face and conquer the better salesperson you'll become. Soon you'll learn to ask questions that actually flush out objections or even eliminate them.

As a salesperson who is truly interested in your clients' success, you don't want to leave them with unvoiced objections, do you? Wouldn't you rather they bring them up so you can address them? If you can fix a part of your proposal so your client will be more comfortable, wouldn't you want to know about it?

Try to Eliminate Objections Before They Come Up

Do your homework. Call on the people who are likely to benefit from your product at the time you want them to use it and who can afford to buy it. A lot of this is common sense. Sometimes the objection is that the prospect has no need for your product and no money to buy it. If he or she has no interest or need, you really don't have a prospect, do you? Sometimes in our passion to get in front of a lot of prospects, we don't think and plan well. Remember, you don't get paid to make sales calls. You get paid to make sales. Be particular with how you spend your time.

Bring up the objections yourself. This makes it clear that you are confident of the issue and have no concerns about discussing it. You can apply these ideas to anything you sell, but for the sake of example, suppose you are selling television advertising time to clients, and you anticipate an objection regarding price. You may say, "Some new clients are concerned about what they perceive is the high cost of television advertising. Is that a concern of yours as well?"

When an Objection Is Introduced

Always agree with your client. If you don't, he or she will get angry and defensive and the sale will be over. Agree to the point by saying, "I can understand why you think that" or "I see your point. How about if we…" or "Some of our best customers also had that concern at first."

Listen intently and let the client speak. We often think of our rebuttal when a client voices an objection rather than really listen to what the client has to say. Worse, we often interrupt before the client finishes, assuming we know where he or she is going. This is not only rude, but we are often wrong, and what we think the client was going to say might not be true at all. Listen not with the intent to rebut but to understand. Your clients should never feel you are going to argue with them. They want to know you truly understand how they feel, and you <u>should</u> truly understand how they feel. Don't proceed until you do.

Restate the objection. Paraphrasing can clear up any misunderstanding about what you think you heard and will show the client that you really do want to understand him or her. It also will let you turn the objection into a value statement. Here's an example:

Client: "This costs too much."

You: "If I understand correctly, you're concerned about receiving sufficient value for your investment."

Client: "That's right, I am."

You: "I can certainly understand that. Let's see. How many sales would you have to make to recoup what you might spend on this advertising package?"

Client: "At least ten."

You: "If your commercial is viewed by ten thousand people and your product is advertised at the right time of the year and at the right price, it seems reasonable that you would sell many more than ten. Do you agree?"

Question the objection. Ask the client to elaborate upon his or her point. You may hear that something you said was misunderstood, and you can clear up the point and get it out of the way.

Uncover the Real Objection by Playing "What If?" To answer an objection successfully, you need to know what it really is. Sometimes clients are hesitant to tell you why they really object, or they may not know themselves, so they just throw something out because they don't want to commit. Here's an example:

Client: "I don't have a commercial produced that I could air right now."

You: "I see. If you did have a commercial produced, would you agree that this is a good time for you to make an investment that will lead to more sales?"

Client: "Not really. I don't have enough product in stock to advertise right now. My stock will be replenished in about three weeks."

You: "Well, certainly timing is everything. Meanwhile, suppose we get a commercial produced so we can be ready when you have product you want to move?"

Clarify and confirm. Clarify that you have answered the objection, and ask the client to tell you that it is no longer a concern. If the client does that, it's time to restate the benefits of going ahead and ask for the order.

> Remember that objections are opportunities to discover what may be standing in the way of the sale and to address and solve the issue and move on to "Sold!"
>
> Welcome objections!

Delivering Bad News

No one likes to be the bearer of bad news. If you are a manager or executive, however, this task almost certainly will fall upon you at one time or another. Lee Iacocca, former chairman and CEO of Chrysler said, "Tell it first. Tell it straight. Tell it all." Here are some additional strategies for delivering bad news:

1. **Get it over with.** If the people to whom you are delivering the bad news know it's coming, they'll be annoyed if you stretch it out with fake conversation, asking them about their weekends, for example. Needless conversation also will make you seem unsure of yourself and may have the listener pushing you to change your mind.
2. **Be direct, but use tact and choose your words carefully.** A truly sincere delivery helps people feel less angry.
3. **Say what you need to say and then be quiet.** If you go on and on defending or justifying the decision, you'll appear as though you are unsure whether the right decision has been made. You'll give away your authority if you justify too much. Once you've said what you needed to say, be patient and compassionate.

4. **Allow time to hear the person out.** Listening attentively and showing genuine empathy (without seeming indecisive) is critically important. If the bad news involves a person losing their job, no matter how true it is that a person's performance is not the reason for the termination, most people will believe that if they had done a better job, they would not have been displaced. Their self-worth may have taken a beating. Avoid saying that you know how they feel. The truth is that you don't know.

5. **If the news is regarding a displacement, even though these people may get a generous severance package, this would not be the time to mention that things could be worse.** If you put yourself in their shoes, you'll know that this is a time of great stress and anxiety, no matter what the severance package offers.

6. **Delivering bad news over the telephone is almost as bad as delivering it in an e-mail.** People feel disrespected if they think their manager doesn't have the time to meet with them.

The best outcome you can hope for is that people understand and know from your past behavior that you have concern and respect for them. Trust your instincts.

Elevator Speeches: You've Got Thirty Seconds

How often do you miss opportunities to interest prospective clients because you can't clearly and concisely describe what you do and how you could benefit them? If this has happened to you, resolve now to spend some time developing an effective elevator speech.

Elevator speeches are short, clear, interest-generating messages. The term "elevator speech" was coined to describe a scenario in which you step into an elevator with a prospective client and must interest him or her and reach your goal in the time it takes to travel a few floors.

We live in a headline society. If you can't say it in thirty seconds, you probably can't say it at all. Your goal should be to:

- catch them

- keep them

- convince them

Elevator speeches are used when meeting prospective clients, writing introductory e-mails or letters, leaving messages on a prospect's answering machine, introducing yourself at networking events, or anytime someone asks, "What do you do?"

Crafting Your Message

An elevator speech is a mini-presentation and, as such, should follow the same guidelines as any effective presentation.

1. **Consider the audience.** Develop different messages depending on who is listening. A generic elevator speech is sure to fail.
2. **Determine your goal.** What do you want as a result of having described your business? An appointment? A referral?
3. **Logically lay out your main points.** Your main points should include who you are, what you do, who you do it for, what the results are, and how you can benefit the listener.
4. **Close by asking for action.** Ask for what you want (your goal).

The most important thing to remember about presenting your elevator speech is the following:

Ask yourself why an individual should have an interest in what you have to say. If you let that thought guide you, you will develop a compelling elevator speech.

> **It is not about you.
> It is about them.**

1. Have an intriguing first sentence. Catch them! Example: "I can save your company a lot of money."
2. Your message should be written in the way you talk, in clear, everyday language.
3. Avoid industry jargon.
4. Go for brevity and clarity. Write out your message and then eliminate any unnecessary words.
5. Don't tell everything. Your purpose is to intrigue your listener to have them want more. Keep them!
6. Develop different versions of your message based on the audiences you encounter. You should have a ten-second message, a thirty-second message, and a two-minute message. You could have one version of your ten-second message for a prospective client and another for a social occasion where people are likely to ask about your profession.
   The ten-second version includes:

- an intriguing first sentence

- one simple sentence about what you do or provide

- clearly stated benefits of your product or service

- a request for action

The thirty-second version includes all of the above, but before the request for action, add:

- your company's qualifications

- your company's goals

The two-minute version includes all of the above, but before the request for action, add a success story.

Samples

Here are some samples of elevator speeches for Wheless-Wyatt Communications, which serves business professionals with executive coaching, speech coaching, presentation skills training, and custom addresses:

1. "We help business professionals reach their communications potential. Many business people stumble through meetings, fail to gain commitment, make ineffective sales calls, and put clients and audiences to sleep. Effective communicators and skilled presenters get things done, which contributes directly to your bottom line. I'd like to see if there's a fit between what we do and any needs you may have. Can we set a time to meet next week?"

2. "The reason I wanted to see you is because chances are that you will attend a meeting today or in the near future that will waste your time. We work with business professionals to develop the skills to be effective communicators so when they speak up in a meeting or step in front of an audience, no one's time is wasted. What a money-saver that is. I'd like to tell you more about how we've helped companies like yours. Could I call your office on Monday to work out a time?"

3. "In all of my experience, I've never known a company that wouldn't benefit from what we do. We help business professionals reach their communications potential. When people become effective communicators and presenters, they make things happen. Meetings are more valuable. There are fewer mistakes and misunderstandings. Sales increase, and the image of the organization to prospective customers is enhanced when a skilled presenter represents the company. I'd like to learn about your organization and see if we can make a difference for you. Could we get together one day next week?"

Delivering Your Message

- You should be able to deliver your words without sounding scripted, rehearsed, or memorized. Strive to be conversational and natural. Be who you really are.

- What you say should reflect the passion you feel about what you do. Smile. Speak energetically and with conviction. If you can't find anything positive about what you do, an elevator speech will be of little help.

- Practice your message out loud. You'll probably need to edit it several times until it feels right. Have someone role-play it with you.

- Maintain eye contact with the listener.

- Remember to practice often. Otherwise your message may slip from your memory just when you have a perfect opportunity to use it.

In Conclusion

Every interaction you have with another person leaves that person with an impression. Your elevator speech will either have them yawning or wanting to hear more. Isn't it worth spending some time now to make sure you are prepared?

Listening Strategies

I know you hear me, but are you listening?

There are four listening behaviors that, if mastered, I believe will put you in the top 1 percent of leaders, colleagues, parents, spouses, and friends—human beings—who truly know how to listen. Very few people are good listeners.

The first strategy is that you must *choose* to listen. I know how simple that sounds, but the truth is that we constantly—either consciously or subconsciously—make the decision whether to listen. Our decisions can have long-term effects.

If you see someone coming into your office, and your experience has been that the person never really has anything important to say, you may make the choice to act as if you are listening but be completely disengaged. If, however, you make the conscious choice to listen—to really listen—one or two things may happen:

1. You just may hear something you should know.
2. More important, the person leaves your office feeling respected and heard and is likely to model that behavior to someone else.

153

Really listening involves your ears, eyes, heart, and mind. Be completely in the moment. Don't multitask while someone is talking to you. Resist the urge to glance out your door to see who's walking by. Even fiddling with a paperclip can make you appear impatient and disengaged. When someone is talking with you over lunch or in a crowded room, ensure that your eye contact remains fixed on the speaker. Too often we look around to see who else may be there.

If the person catches you at a bad time, say so. For example you might say, "I really want to be able to listen to what you're saying, but right now I'm up against a deadline. Can we talk this afternoon at two o'clock?"

The second listening strategy is to paraphrase. Repeat in your own words what you understood the speaker to say. You'll be amazed at the misunderstandings you'll avoid. You may say, "Let me make sure I understand. You said (or you feel)..." The speaker may say, "No, that isn't at all what I meant" or "Yes, that's it exactly."

When you paraphrase what someone said, you avoid misunderstandings and the speaker feels heard and respected. Often what is said and what is heard are two different things. Paraphrasing can clear up misunderstandings before they go too far. Here's a story to illustrate my point.

That's What I Said, But Not What I Meant

A pastor was trying to raise money to build a wing on his church and was looking for donations. He said to the congregation, "Whoever will get this started by donating the first one thousand dollars gets to choose three hymns."

A woman in the back row stood up and said, "I will, Pastor. I will donate one thousand dollars."

"Thank you so much," responded the Pastor. "Now you can pick three hymns."

The woman looked out over the congregation and, pointing her finger at her targets, said, "I'll take him and him and him."

The third listening strategy is to listen with the intent to report. Imagine how effective your listening would be if you listened with the idea that you had to repeat all the details accurately at a later time.

Many people have trouble remembering names. If we all listened with the intent to report, it would eliminate that problem. Instead, we would actually "hear" the name in the first place, particularly if we knew we had to turn around and introduce the person to someone else.

Combining this strategy with paraphrasing will eliminate errors and miscommunications will be avoided.

Taking notes can be a valuable backup; however, it is easy to slip into a habit of letting our note-taking replace actual listening.

The fourth and final listening strategy is to seek first to understand, then to be understood. This may be the most important listening strategy of all. It comes from Stephen R. Covey's *The 7 Habits of Highly Effective People.* Too often, in our effort to be heard, instead of listening—really listening—to the speaker, we're thinking of what our response will be. Sometimes we even develop the habit of interrupting and finishing the speaker's sentences for him or her, which often takes the conversation in a completely different direction.

Listen to understand not only the words, but also the feelings behind the words, to "feel" from the speaker's perspective. Put yourself in his or her shoes. Consider what is *not* being said in addition to what *is* being said. Only then can your response accurately reflect that you have completely understood.

Not seeking first to understand can lead us to make assumptions, and that can cause misunderstandings, as it did for the businessman in the next story.

Excuse Me, Sir?

A woman was selling apples on the streets of New York City. Every day a businessman on his way to his office would pass by and, without any conversation, drop a quarter into her basket and not take an apple. This went on day after day, month after month.

One day as he passed by, the woman called after him, "Sir, sir..."

He turned and said, "I know. You want to know why I drop a quarter in your basket day after day and not take an apple."

"No, sir," she replied. "I want to tell you that the apples have gone up to thirty-five cents."

If you adopt these four listening strategies—all of them or even just one of them—you'll be among an elite group of people who truly listen. This will benefit not only you, but also everyone around you.

Multitasking: Scattering Thoughts and Efforts

Is it better to do one thing well or several things poorly?

The term "multitasking" was born in the 1960s when engineers learned that computers could do more than one thing at a time. Since then it seems we've decided that people should be more like machines, and we tax ourselves to see how many things we can do at once without blowing up.

Some people think of multitasking as a skill. Their office doors are open. Their business BlackBerrys and personal cell phones are on. The fax machine is running. Their desktop computer and laptop are both on. They're talking to someone on the phone, pretending to listen while putting their hand over the receiver so they can carry on conversations with other people who have walked into their office.

They may think all of this is impressive. They give the impression of being incredibly busy. If you're doing more than one thing at a time, however, you're doing neither of them well. Our brains are just not wired that way.

A 2001 University of Michigan study showed that chronic multitasking has roughly the same effect on the brain as a few strong martinis. It can lead to short-term memory loss, hypertension, slower reflexes, insomnia, mental fatigue, and impaired judgment. But if you try to explain to unrepentant multitaskers that they may be wasting half their day hopping from one thing to another, perhaps endangering others along the way, they won't listen; they'll be too busy. Therein lies the genius of multitasking, because in its purest form, multitasking is nothing more than the art of looking busy while accomplishing absolute squat.

Think of how much more effective and productive you could be if you could stay in the moment and concentrate on one thing at a time. Think of how much more respect you'll show the people who are talking to you if you give them your full attention.

I'm a realist. I know that in this fast-paced world multitasking is sometimes necessary. I also know that many times it isn't necessary. When making the decision whether to multitask at any given moment, be aware of what multitasking does to your focus, your competence, your accuracy, and your productivity.

Focusing on one thing at a time takes effort and discipline, but it definitely pays off. Try it for a week. You'll be amazed at how much more you'll get done and how often you'll get it right the first time.

Small Talk: How to Survive It, Benefit From It, and Even Enjoy It

Most of us hate the idea of making small talk. We think of it as shallow and a waste of our time. Some people are even intimidated by it. Why? To understand why we feel the way we do, it's important to think about how we were raised.

- We were told never to talk to strangers.

- We were told it's impolite to speak without being properly introduced.

- We were told that good things come to he who waits.

- We were told it's better to be safe than sorry (in other words, we might get rejected).

No wonder we aren't eager to rush into a room of people we don't know and start chatting away.

What about the *advantages* of being able to talk with anyone at anytime? The ability to connect with people through small talk is an acquired skill, and it can be learned just like any other skill, but first you must see the value in it.

A Stanford University School of Business study tracked MBAs ten years after they graduated. It seems their grade point averages had no bearing on their success, but their ability to converse with others did.

(See http://www.cnn.com/2005/US/Careers/03/03/small.talk/index.html)

The ability to converse effectively with others is the mark of real leadership in taking the lead to get to know people. Consider that any interaction you have with another person leaves that person with an impression, and the initial impression is a lasting one. Remember, you don't get a second chance to make a good first impression.

None of us wants to be wrong. As I mentioned earlier, if someone's initial impression is that you are warm, friendly, and smart, and the next time they see you, your behavior is cold, aloof, and rude, they are more likely to let it pass, thinking you are just having a bad day. On the other hand, if you behaved that way at the first meeting, and then subsequently came across as warm, caring, and friendly, the person would be inclined to think you are being fake. It takes a long time to change a first impression. This is why it is so important for people to see the real you the first time.

How Does One Acquire the Skill of Making Small Talk?

1. **You must be convinced that your appearance at the event is of some benefit to you**. If you drag yourself there feeling that you're wasting your time, it will come across in your demeanor. You'll be remembered that way, and you would have been better off not showing up at all. Some benefits of being at an event could be:

- You may spend some casual time with people who work with or for you and get to know them better. You also can help them know more about you as a person.

- The host is a valuable client and will appreciate your support in being there.

- Your spouse is the host or hostess and will appreciate your support in being there.

- You may meet someone who can help you acquire or do something that is important to you. Small talk can lead to big talk and big opportunities.

- You may learn something.

- You just may have fun.

2. **Know how you will introduce yourself**. When someone asks what you do, have your thirty-second elevator speech so committed to memory that you

won't have to conjure it up. Describe what you do in clear, everyday language that offers a clear explanation. Instead of saying, "I'm the head of the healthcare financial services division of America's Bank," say, "I'm with America's Bank. Our division helps businesses in the healthcare industry with their financial needs and brings them the products, services, and capital they need to operate."

3. **Know how to open a conversation**. You can do that by commenting on something you and the listener obviously have in common, such as the place where you are meeting or knowing the host or hostess. Here are some examples.

Example 1

You: "This event seems to be getting bigger and bigger every year. Have you been here before?"

Charles: "Yes."

You: "What do you think has kept it growing all these years?" (To encourage more conversation, ask open-ended questions that require more than a "yes" or "no").

Suppose in answer to your question "Have you been here before?" Charles says, "No." You could say, "Well, I think you'll enjoy it. They always do a good job of showcasing their accomplishments. What do you do, Charles?"

Example 2

You: "It's nice to meet you, Steve. How do you know David and Mary?"

Steve: "They were our neighbors back in Cleveland."

You: "Cleveland? Do you still live there?"

And the conversation takes off from there.

Listen intently when someone tells you his or her name. The main reason many of us don't remember names is that we never "heard" or "registered" the name in the first place. Repeat the person's name and "work" with it. For example you might say, "Steven Jordan? Is that spelled S-t-e-v-e-n or S-t-e-p-h-e-n?" Repeat the name frequently during the conversation.

Example 3

You're at an after-hours event with your team. You may start a conversation by saying, "Well, it's been a long week. What will you do this weekend for fun, Janet?" Janet says, "I love to work in my garden, and I have a lot of catching up to do." There you go. You may have never known that about Janet if it weren't for small talk.

4. **You must have something to say**. Being well read and keeping abreast of current events are keys to interesting conversation. Be sure to avoid anything controversial, political, or too personal. You always can ask someone about their family, their occupation, or what they do for recreation. Then **listen**. Really

listen. Be careful not to look around the room when someone is speaking to you. Doing so says loudly and clearly, *I wonder if anyone is here who is more important or interesting than you.* Maintain eye contact. If you listen carefully, what you hear will provide you with more information to keep the conversation going. Resist the temptation to think of your response while the other person is talking. Listen all the way to the end of his or her sentence(s).

5. **You must be genuinely interested in other people**. When you come across as confident, warm, and friendly, it puts the other person at ease, and it will have the same effect on you. Remember that people will forget what you said and what you did, but **they will never forget how you made them feel**.

As tempting as it is to remain with one person who is easy to talk with, manners dictate that you move on to others. When doing so, you should have something planned to say that will have the person you are leaving know you were into the conversation. You may say, "It was good to meet you, Bob. I'm really interested in that new wing you're planning for the hospital. Let's stay in touch" or "I've really enjoyed talking with you, Alice. The next time you go through Tennessee, be sure to look up that fly-fishing spot I told you about." (Refer back to your discussion.)

You can leave the event knowing that you were important to the people you approached and with whom you conversed, perhaps in just making them feel more comfortable, which can be a big deal to many people. You will be well remembered and appreciated.

Determine your positive attitude, grab your business cards, plan your introduction, have something to say, be truly interested, and really listen. The rest will take care of itself.

Conference Calls
Oh, good! An opportunity to catch up on my e-mail!

If you're reading this between the hours of seven a.m. and six p.m., most likely there are, at this moment, hundreds, perhaps thousands, of worthless meetings taking place across the country. The invention of conference calls has allowed an unlimited number of otherwise productive people to be included in the worthless meetings.

Conference calls were intended to save money by saving travel expenses and the time associated with travel. Too often, however, conference calls:

- are not well planned

- are not well thought out

- are not well conducted

- include people who are not needed, taking them away from what they're paid to do

How can that possibly save money? According to Russell Research, Inc., 47 percent of people surveyed felt conference calls were a waste of time and money. I suspect that number is much lower than the actual figure, because almost all of the people I talk with feel that way.

When people are together in a room, civility requires at least the appearance of interest in the speaker's remarks. No such requirement exists during a conference call. We are freed from polite behavior without offending the speaker and often without missing anything important. So instead of listening, we are multitasking.

Again, according to Russell Research, Inc., during conference calls:

- 70 percent of participants work on other company-related projects

- 51 percent read or send e-mail

- 36 percent talk to someone else

- 27 percent surf the Internet

As much as we believe we can, we cannot do two things at once and do either well.

There are companies that have developed software that will alert a conference call leader when some reportable activity is taking place by the "participants", such as answering e-mail, instant messaging, or surfing the web, but I believe that strategy treats the symptoms and not the disease.

The reason people aren't paying attention is because **the call is of no value to them.** I don't blame them for finding something more productive to do.

The value of a conference call to those in attendance is **the responsibility of the call leader.** The leader is responsible for capturing and keeping the attention of those on the call. The guidelines that follow, along with proper planning by the leader, will help ensure that no one's time is wasted—and what a money saver that will be.

Guidelines for Leaders of Effective Conference Calls

1. **Know exactly what the call is to accomplish and who should be involved to achieve the goal.** Keep the number of participants to only those needed. Avoid having anyone on the call who has nothing to contribute or who will not gain value from the time invested.

2. **Send out an agenda well in advance.** Let everyone know what they are expected to contribute.

3. **Run your conference call as you would any effective meeting.** Begin the call on time. Stick to the time allotted for your agenda items. If other topics come up, address them at the end of the call if there is time. If not, schedule another call to discuss them. Your audiences will learn that they can count on you to be disciplined and respectful of their time.

4. **Make a good first impression.** The impression you make in the first thirty to sixty seconds of a conference call will determine whether your audience decides to listen. Speak with energy in your voice, and use vocal inflection to emphasize key points. Avoid, at all costs, delivering a boring monologue. Keep everyone engaged.

5. **Enunciate clearly and control your speech rate.**

6. **If you use visuals, include only one clearly illustrated point per slide.** Otherwise the slide will cease to do its job of keeping your listeners on point and will become a distraction. When you are no longer referring to the visual, put up a plain slide that states, "This portion of the call is audio only. Please give your attention to the speaker."

7. **Keep your calls short (less than thirty minutes) and to the point.** Do not ramble. You should have rehearsed and have a bulleted outline of what you want to say.

8. **Let those on your call know whether to interrupt with questions or to hold their questions until the end.** Each person, even though they feel everyone should recognize their voice, should identify themselves each time they speak.

9. **Before ending the call, restate the main points, the expected next steps, and who is responsible for what.**

10. Send minutes or notes of what took place in the call to all participants within twenty-four hours. You, as the leader, should not try to wear too many hats. Have someone else be responsible for capturing the meeting in notes and sending them out. If it isn't worth the time to send out the minutes, reconsider whether the call was necessary.

If you follow these guidelines, you'll gain the reputation of conducting disciplined calls that are of value to your listeners. Rather than planning what else they are going to do during your call, they will be clearing their desks and their minds to give you their full attention.

For the Conference Call Audience

Are you constantly asked to participate in calls that waste your time? Let me suggest the following:

Me: "I'd like for you to be on my conference call Thursday at three p.m."

You: "I'd be happy to, Sherry. What would you like the call to accomplish, and how can I contribute?"

If I don't know what I want the call to accomplish or what I want you to contribute, I'll stop asking you to participate, which is exactly what you'd want me to do if my calls are typically a waste of time.

E-mail

Hold everything! I got a "bing"!

E-mail was a great idea. It was intended to:

- get short notes out quickly

- get the same message to multiple recipients simultaneously and instantly

- save time and money on paper, printing, and postage

E-mail, however, is not being used as it was intended. Just as with PowerPoint and conference calls, something has gone horribly wrong.

- E-mail is used when another form of communication would be more effective or efficient.

- E-mail is sent to people who have no need to receive it (CC, BCC, "Reply to All").

- E-mail is often poorly written, which causes misunderstandings.

- E-mail usually contains too much information or unnecessary attachments.

- E-mail allows senders to feel we are constantly reachable or interruptible and that they can expect an immediate answer from us. (We encourage this by actually being constantly reachable or interruptible!)

Another problem with e-mail is the sheer volume of it. When we first began working together, one of my executive coaching clients received more than four hundred e-mails a day. How could she possibly have time for anything else?

The Intel Corporation reports that one-third of all e-mail is unnecessary. Russell Research, Inc. reports that when we turn our attention away from what we are doing to attend to e-mail, it takes roughly twenty-four minutes for us to get back to what we were doing. How many times a day can you afford that kind of distraction?

No one talks to each other anymore. More than 50 percent of e-mail is sent to people in the same office. Often they are so close together that they share a four-foot-high wall between their cubicles. Yet instead of speaking directly to each other and gaining an immediate answer or resolving an issue, they send e-mails back and forth for days.

There is a movement underway for companies to ban internal e-mail. Imagine that scenario in your organization. Would it be a good thing or a bad thing?

What can we do to make e-mail more efficient and effective? Let's start by controlling the volume of it. You're probably wondering how you can control how much e-mail is sent to you. Studies show that for every e-mail you send, you get two in return. So if you want to reduce your e-mail, follow this guideline:

Send less. Get less.

Before writing any e-mail, consider these four questions:

1. Is this e-mail necessary?
2. Is this e-mail worth the interruption it will cause the recipient?
3. Is it necessary that I copy anyone?
4. Is e-mail the right medium for this message?

I offer some guidelines below to improve your e-mail communication. First, however, let's explore number four above, "Is e-mail the right medium for this message?" Consider that the state of mind you are in when you write an e-mail may not match the state of mind the recipient is in when he or she receives it. Your message will pass through the person's biases, prejudices, and mood at the time he or she reads it. Because your words don't have the benefit of facial expression or vocal inflection to help the reader know what you *mean* by what you write, misunderstandings can occur.

Consider the following sentence:

I didn't say you did it.

Read the sentence aloud, each time emphasizing a different word. Suddenly this sentence can have multiple meanings.

Always read your messages from your reader's point of view. It's best to avoid messages that convey feelings; stick to just the facts. Pick up the phone or sit down face-to-face if you don't want to be misunderstood.

Practical Guidelines Before You Hit "Send"

1. **As with any communication, have a goal.** What do you want this message to accomplish? Include only the information that is needed to reach your goal, and send the message only to those people who need to be involved.

2. **Use the CC (copy) field sparingly.** Only include those who need to receive the message. Early in your message, explain to those copied why they are being copied. Is it for information only? Are they to respond or take some action?

3. **Use the BCC (blind copy) field when you have multiple addressees to keep your recipients' e-mail addresses private.** It may be a good idea to let your reader know that you have sent your e-mail to others. For example you might write,

"I'm sending this to you and to other clients because I would like your ideas." Consider that using the blind copy field typically means you wish to keep the fact from your addressee that you are also sending the message to someone else. Should you handle the situation differently? What would happen if your addressee learned of the BCC? ("Why did you BCC my boss on this?")

4. **Do not use "Reply to All" unless everyone needs to see your response.**

5. **Use the subject line to describe the purpose and content of your message.** The subject line should be like a headline in a newspaper. It should intrigue the reader to open the message and learn more.

6. **When responding to an e-mail, change the subject line.** Should you need to find a particular message later, a conversation that goes on and on with the same subject line will make finding that message much harder than it needs to be. Update the subject line with each message.

   When your message is really short, for example, "I will meet you at nine a.m.," consider putting the entire message in the subject line, followed by the words "end of message." If you don't include "end of message," your reader may write back and tell you there is nothing in the body of your e-mail.

7. **The first paragraph should contain all the important information—the purpose of the message and what is contained in the body.** Many people don't read beyond the first paragraph unless given a reason to continue.

8. **Be succinct.** Use short sentences and paragraphs. Use lists and bullet points for clarity.

9. **Your message should preempt further questions by answering them upfront.** You could go on and on for days with an e-mail string about which day to meet for lunch, where, and what time if you send an e-mail that asks, "Can we meet for lunch this week?" Instead eliminate all the back and forth by asking, "Can we meet for lunch at noon on Tuesday at the Four Seasons?"

10. **When you receive an e-mail with many questions, insert your answers immediately behind each question, using a different color font.** Cut and paste the entire message back to the sender. Have you ever received a response a week after sending an e-mail, and it said, "Yes, that will be fine," but you can't recall what your question was? The above suggestion will eliminate that problem.

11. **Whenever possible paste attachments into the body of the message.** Some attachments can't be opened on handheld devices.

12. **Do not type in all CAPITAL LETTERS.**

13. **Use proper spelling, grammar, and punctuation.** Avoid acronyms and texting abbreviations such as "OMG" or "LOL."

14. **Do not overuse the "high priority," "urgent," or "important" notations.**

15. **Read your message from your recipient's point of view.** Let your message sit for a bit before you send it. Reread it to make sure it is clear. Fill in the address line last so you don't accidently send the message before you're ready.

16. **Never, never, never send an e-mail when you're angry (or, as someone in an audience in Tampa added, when you're drunk!).**

Remember that your messages are dated, timed records that are tied directly to you. They will be around long after you believe they have been deleted. Don't get personal. This is business. Stay on the subject. Keep it professional. Never write in an e-mail anything you wouldn't want to see printed in the newspaper. You have a responsibility to keep your company (and your future) protected. The best advice is "When in doubt, don't."

Part 5 - Getting Started

Many goals are never attained, not because they cease being important, but more often because of a failure to take the first step.

> *"The best way to predict the future is to create it."*
>
> —Peter Drucker,
> author and management consultant

Don't wait until you are ready to put yourself and your ideas out there. Work from where you are with what you have.

> *"Do not wait; the time will never be just right. Start where you stand, and work with whatever tools you may have at your command, and better tools will be found as you go along."*
>
> —George Herbert,
> British poet

You are most likely surrounded by competent colleagues you can call on to give you feedback and help keep you accountable to achieve the goals you've set for yourself.

If you spend some time learning about your current skill level and address any areas that need improvement one at a time until they are no longer issues, you will be well on your way to being an exceptional communicator. Use the assessment tools in this section of the book to help you evaluate and develop your communication skills.

Nothing will affect your career more, positively or negatively, than the manner in which you communicate.

There is no better teacher than experience. So get out there!

Personal Skills Development Plan

You cannot address everything at once. Identify and concentrate on one skill at a time to improve your communication skills. Once you have mastered a skill, move on to another one. This plan will help you stay on track and stay the course.

Visual

Appearance: Do you appear professional? Well groomed? Well dressed? Do you make a positive first impression?

Demeanor: Are you confident? Energetic? Personable? Engaging? Comfortable? Do you come across as passionate? Knowledgeable? Convincing? Honest? Likeable? Authoritative?

Body Language: Do you make good eye contact? Do you use facial expressions effectively? Do you use your hands effectively? Do you use appropriate movement? Do you stand up straight with your head held up?

Vocal

Sound of Your Voice: Is it strong? Confident? Clear? Interesting? Do you use inflection effectively? Do you effectively use pauses? Is your voice conversational? How would you rate your pace, volume, and enunciation?

Verbal

Your Message: Is your message designed to achieve a clear goal? Is it organized? Easy to follow? Logical? Concise? Persuasive? Interesting? Anecdotal? Do you provide stories and examples? Do you use everyday, understandable language and a strong, engaging opening? Do you have a summarizing and directive close?

Goals:_____

_____

_____

_____

_____

_____

_____

_____

Preparation Checklist

In real estate the mantra is "Location, location, location." In presenting it's "Preparation, preparation, preparation." While I believe you can over-rehearse, I don't believe you can over-prepare. The items that follow will help you dot the i's and cross the t's. You may want to amend this list so it's applicable to your assignment(s).

Once you have checked off everything on this list, go to your presentation and enjoy yourself!

Audience

☐ Who are they? What do you know about their company, their product, and their problems?

☐ What are their jobs and skill levels?

☐ What are their ages?

☐ What is their gender?

☐ What is their education level?

☐ What do they already know about your subject?

☐ How do they feel about you, your company, and your point of view?

☐ Where are they likely to disagree with you?

☐ What level of detail do they want—general or very specific?

☐ Will spouses or others be present?

☐ How many people will be in the audience?

☐ How will they be dressed?

☐ If they are attending a convention, is there a specific theme you could tie into?

Other:

_____

_____

_____

Meeting Site Details

☐ What is the room like where you will be presenting?

☐ How will the audience be seated?

☐ Will you need sound amplification? Will you have a fixed microphone or a lavaliere microphone? Will you be turning it on and off or will someone else control it?

☐ Will the audience be eating while you are speaking?

☐ Is there likely to be distracting noise from an adjacent room?

☐ Will other people speak before or after you?

☐ Will you be on a stage or riser?

☐ Will there be a lectern? If not, where will you place your notes?

☐ Where will you be seated before you are introduced? Can you make your way easily to the lectern?

☐ Will you need a laptop or a PowerPoint projector? Will the projector be in the ceiling or on a table?

☐ Will you advance your own slides or will someone else do that?

☐ If you're bringing your own equipment, will you need extension cords and tape to tape them down?

☐ When can you rehearse your presentation in the presentation room with the equipment you will be using and with anyone who may be helping you?

☐ Will the lighting prevent you from your seeing your notes clearly?

☐ Will someone introduce you? Do you need to pre-pare the introduction?

☐ What time will the audience arrive?

☐ If you have handouts to give the audience afterward, where will you put them?

☐ Do you know exactly how to get to the meeting site? Is there an alternate route in case of a traffic jam? Should you travel the night before?

☐ Do you need to mail any materials in advance and to whom? Who will deliver them to the site?

☐ Do you have the name and contact information for the site contact in a place where you can easily find it once you leave your home or office?

Other:

_____

_____

_____

Your Message

☐ Do you have a clear goal? If you're successful, what will happen as a result of your presentation?

☐ Have you considered your message from your audience's point of view? What's in it for them?

☐ Have you thought of every conceivable question or objection your audience could have and how you will answer them?

☐ Do you have a strong, engaging open that grabs your audience's attention?

☐ Is your message logically laid out, including only the information that will help you achieve your goal?

☐ Do you have a strong, summarizing, and directive close?

☐ Have you considered how, or if, you will entertain questions?

☐ Have you considered where visuals may aid your audience and make your presentation clearer and more interesting?

☐ If you're using an easel and pad, have you practiced any drawings to make sure they fit properly on the page? Do you have the right markers with backups?

☐ Have you rehearsed your presentation out loud, using any equipment you will need and timing it out to about 20 percent less time than you have been allotted?

☐ Have you thought of what might go wrong and how you will handle it?

☐ Do you have backup copies of your notes and/or slides?

Other:

_____

_____

_____

Presentation Day

☐ Do you feel comfortable and confident in what you chose to wear?

☐ Does your appearance match the image you intend to project?

☐ Do you have a backup plan? A clean shirt and tie in case you spill coffee on yourself? A spare pair of stockings in case you get a run? Another pair of shoes in case you break a heel? A spare pair of eyeglasses in case you have trouble with your contacts? Medications you may need if you feel a headache coming on?

☐ Do you have a handkerchief or tissue?

☐ Do you have room-temperature water nearby (not sitting on the lectern) in case you need it while you are speaking?

☐ After your presentation, spend some time reflecting. What went well? What didn't go so well? What would you do differently next time?

Other:

_____

_____

_____

Recommended Reading

Good presenting is good communication. Because communication accounts for more than 90 percent of what you do, you will find reading materials on this list that may not deal specifically with presentation but with the broader subject of who you are, how you come across, and how you influence people.

Books
101 Secrets of Highly Effective Speakers
by Caryl Rae Krannich

The 7 Habits of Highly Effective People
by Stephen R. Covey

Are You Communicating? by Donald Walton

Crucial Conversations by Kerry Patterson, et al.

Emotional Intelligence by Daniel Goleman

Fire Away by Myles Martel

First Impressions by Ann Demarais and Valerie White

Good to Great by Jim Collins

How to Be Prepared to Think on Your Feet
by Stephen C. Rafe

Life Is a Series of Presentations by Tony Jeary

Listening Leaders
by Lyman K. Steil and Richard K. Bommelje

The Overnight Guide to Public Speaking
by Ed Wohlmuth

Real Leaders Don't Do PowerPoint by Christopher Witt

Talking from 9 to 5 by Deborah Tannen

Winning with the News Media by Clarence Jones

Words That Work by Frank I. Luntz

You Are the Message by Roger Ailes and Jon Krashaur

You've Got to Be Believed to Be Heard by Bert Decker

Everyone Communicates, Few Connect
by John C. Maxwell

Articles

"Death by Information Overload" by Paul Hemp (http://hbr.org/2009/09/death-by-information-overload/ar/1)

"How PowerPoint Downed the Space Shuttle" by Sid Peimer   (http://www.stratplanning.com/sp_study.php?id=study_072)

"PowerPoint Turns 20, as Its Creators Ponder a Dark Side to Success" by L. Gomes (http://online.wsj.com/article/SB118228116940840904.html)

"We Have Met the Enemy and He Is PowerPoint" by Elisabeth Bumiller

(http://www.nytimes.com/2010/04/27/world/27powerpoint.html)

www.ingramcontent.com/pod-product-compliance
Lightning Source LLC
Chambersburg PA
CBHW051455170526
45166CB00001B/256